Studies in applied regional scien

This series in applied regional, urban and
environmental analysis aims to provide
regional scientists with a set of adequate tools
for empirical regional analysis and for practical
regional planning problems. The major
emphasis in this series will be upon the
applicability of theories and methods in the
field of regional science; these will be
presented in a form which can be readily used
by practitioners. Both new applications of
existing knowledge and newly developed ideas
will be published in the series

Studies in applied regional science Vol. 3

Estimation of stochastic input-output models

Some statistical problems

S. D. Gerking
Assistant Professor of Economics,
Arizona State University

Martinus Nijhoff Social Sciences Division
Leiden 1976

ISBN 90 207 0628 4

Photoset in Malta by Interprint (Malta) Ltd.

Printed in the Netherlands

To my wife, Janet,
and to our parents

Preface

This monograph is a revision of my Indiana University doctoral dissertation which was completed in April, 1975. Thanks are, therefore, due to the members of my doctoral committee: Saul Pleeter (Chairman), David J. Behling, R. Jeffery Green, Richard L. Pfister, and Elmus Wicker for their helpful comments on previous versions of the manuscript. In addition, I am indebted to the Division of Research and to the Office of Research and Advanced Studies at Indiana University for financial support. As the reader will observe, the techniques developed in Chapters 3 and 4 of this monograph are illustrated using input-output data from West Virginia. These data were generously made available by William H. Miernyk, Director of the Regional Research Institute at West Virginia University. I also wish to acknowledge the Bureau of Business and Economic Research at Arizona State University for providing two research assistants, Kevin A. Nosbisch and Tom R. Rex, who aided in processing the West Virginia data. A third research assistant, Phillip M. Cano, also worked on this project as part of an independent study program taken under my direction during the spring semester of 1975. Finally, I must thank Mary Holguin and Margaret Shumway who expertly typed the final copy of the manuscript.

Despite the efforts of all the individuals mentioned above, I assume responsibility for any errors which may remain.

SDG

Tempe, Arizona

Contents

List of tables

1. Introduction

Since Leontief's pioneering work in the 1940's, input-output models have achieved great popularity in applied economic analysis. This has occurred largely because researchers have found the input-output approach to be useful in examining a wide range of economic problems. For example, these models in their structural form have been used to trace the flow of goods between industries not only at the regional and national levels but at the interregional and international levels as well.[1] In addition, the reduced form has found many applications in forecasting and in economic impact studies.[2]

In fact, it has been claimed that input-output is the most powerful empirical tool available to economists for analyzing a broad range of problems. Two writers have made this view emphatic. Shortly after input-output models were first developed, a committee, represented by members of the National Security Resources Board, the Council of Economic Advisors, and the Bureau of the Budget, was organized within the Department of Defense. They reported:

'... both in present and in prospect, the interindustry relations study technique is the most efficient and comprehensive technique available for studying the total effects of any program, civilian or military on the economy and upon the several industries of the economy.'[3]

More recently, Richardson restated this position. In particular, he argued:

In the absence of further theoretical advances and the provision of more data the use of more complex econometric forecasting techniques is not yet practicable, ... and input-output models are probably the most useful forecasting tool currently available.[4]

Despite these protestations, though, the 'goodness of fit' between the equations of an input-output model and data from the real world is largely unknown. This is surprising because the ideas of statistical theory are basic to evaluating the performance of economic models. Nevertheless, the problem of calculating standard errors for the parameter estimates in a static, open input-output model has been virtually ignored. In fact, the need for calculating standard errors had seldom been recognized even though input-output models are often implemented from sample rather than census data.

Oversights of this nature have created serious difficulties in interpreting estimated input-output models. This may be illustrated by their use in economic forecasting. To this effect, suppose that this type of model has been estimated for an economic system in the year t. Further, let the estimated version of the structural form of the model be written as

$$X(t) = A X(t) + Y(t) \cdot \tag{1.1}$$

where $X(t)$ is an mxl vector of total outputs in each of m sectors for year t; A is an mxm matrix of estimates for the true matrix of technical coefficients; and $Y(t)$ is an mxl vector containing such exogenous factors as final demands by households and exports. Now, suppose that predictions of the vector $X(t + s), s > 0$, are desired. As is usually the case, assume: (1) $Y(t + s)$ is known (somehow) and (2) the true technical coefficients do not change over time. At this point, the problem is well-defined. Simply put equation (1.1) into reduced form and predict that

$$X(t + s) = (I - A)^{-1} Y(t + s) \tag{1.2}$$

It is commonplace in input-output analysis to interpret equation (1.2) as a deterministic or exact forecast. However, to contend that this forecast of $X(t + s)$ will come true with certainty is optimism to a fault. That is, even if $Y(t + s)$ is known, the estimates in A may be governed by a probability distribution. This might arise, for example, if the data used to construct A were obtained by a non-exhaustive sampling procedure. In this case, then, there would clearly be some uncertainty associated with the prediction of $X(t + s)$. But most importantly, the magnitude of this uncertainty depends critically upon the dispersion of the distribution of A. However, as was indicated previously, measures of dispersion have never been calculated for estimates of the technical coefficients.

Many input-output analysts, though, would probably dismiss this argument as a straw man. After all, they would contend, there is evidence suggesting that the true technical coefficients change substantially over time and it is these fluctuations which are of overriding importance for future investigation. This is certainly a relevant consideration, but it is most germane if the input-output system in (1.1) is interpreted as a set of m accounting identities showing a sector by sector breakdown of total sales for each industry. If this were the case, the elements of A would be unique at a point in time but might be expected to vary over time. It should be emphasized, though, that this is not the usual interpretation of an input-output system. In Leontief's words, this system is '... an attempt to apply the economic theory of general equilibrium – or better, general interdependence – to an empirical study of the interrelations among the different parts of an ... economy...'[5]

It is important, therefore, to inquire as to the correspondence between input-output models and the economic systems they purport to represent. In fact, this question will be systematically explored in the following chapters. Specifically, three objectives will be pursued. First, it will be demonstrated that the current method of estimating technical coefficients is deficient. The second, and most important objective, then, is to show how two-stage least squares (TSLS) may be used to estimate a set of technical coefficients. In particular, it will be argued that if certain assumptions are satisfied, this regression method will produce: (1) statistically consistent estimates of these parameters and (2) asymptotic standard errors for these estimates when applied to cross-sectional data. Hence, judging from this second property, this method should be valuable in determining the accuracy with which input-output models depict actual economic behavior.

As a third, and subordinate objective, three further uses of the TSLS estimation technique will be studied. First of all, current methods for reconciling or combining 'rows only' and 'columns only' estimates of the technical coefficients will be reviewed in order to demonstrate that they are haphazard and may lead to substantial estimation errors. It will then be argued that the following reconciliation procedure is superior: (1) Use TSLS to calculate both types of estimates for each technical coefficient and (2) apply the standard theorems on linear combinations of random variables in order to obtain a minimum variance reconciled estimator.

Second, a method for selecting samples of optimum size in future input-output studies will be described. This method, which closely parallels its counterpart in the literature on stratified sampling, is also based upon the minimum variance principle. Furthermore, this sample selection procedure should prove to be useful in future input-output studies because it specifies the criteria for constructing the most cost-effective input-output table subject to a budget constraint.

Third, and finally, the problem of aggregation bias, which may cause inaccurate forecasts of future total output vectors, will be investigated from a new viewpoint. In this discussion, the size of the aggregation bias will be shown to depend upon the statistical technique used to estimate the technical coefficients. This result will then be used to show how a large part of this source of error may be eliminated simply by choosing the appropriate estimator. As will be emphasized, this property gives input-output analysts much wider flexibility in reducing aggregation bias than is generally realized.

As a matter of organization, the remaining discussion will be divided into five chapters. Chapter 3 will develop the TSLS estimator for the technical coefficients. In addition, this chapter provides an illustration of this technique using cross-sectional data from Miernyk's 1965 study of West Virginia. Chapter 4, then, suggests methods for improving current reconciliation procedures and for obtaining samples of optimum size in future input-output studies. These methods are also illustrated using the West Virginia data. In Chapter 5, the results on reducing aggregation bias will be presented. Finally, Chapter 6 provides a summary and outlines some possible directions for future research. Before any of these tasks can be undertaken, though, some background material must be provided. This will be done in Chapter 2 by reviewing the formal structure of input-output systems and commenting on some tests of these models which the regression approach is designed to replace.

NOTES

1. For example, see Leon Moses, 'The Stability of Interregional Trading Patterns and Input-Output Analysis,' *American Economic Review*, XLV, December, 1955, and Roger Riefler and Charles M. Tiebout, 'Interregional Input-Output: An Empirical California–Washington Model,' *Journal of Regional Science*, X, August, 1970.
2. For example, see Walter Isard and Thomas W. Langford, Jr., 'Impact of the Vietnam War on the Philadelphia Economy,' *Regional Input-Output Study: Recollections, Reflections, and Diverse Notes on the Philadelphia Experience*, Cambridge, Mass., MIT Press, 1971.
3. Ezra Glazer, 'Interindustry Economics Research,' *The American Statistician*, V, April–May, 1951, p. 9.
4. Harry W. Richardson, *Input-Output and Regional Economics*, New York, John Wiley and Sons, 1972, p. 157.
5. Wassily W. Leontief, *The Structure of the American Economy: 1919–1939*, New York, Oxford University Press, 1951, p. 3.

2. Tests of the static, open input-output model: an appraisal

As was pointed out in the introduction, measures of dispersion, such as standard errors, have never been calculated for the estimated coefficients in a cross-sectionally based interindustry model. However, empirical input-output models have been subjected to other types of experiments in order to determine their effectiveness in representing actual economic systems. The purpose of this chapter is to review some of the more widely used experiments with a view toward showing why they have been inconclusive. Specifically, the discussion to follow will provide the groundwork for a more powerful and more comprehensive test of the input-output approach. The material presented in this chapter will be neither comprehensive in its coverage nor detailed in its evaluation. Rather, it is meant to provide a set of ideas which will be expanded in subsequent chapters.

This chapter is divided into four sections. First, the structure and empirical implementation of the static, open input-output model will be described. Second, the leading studies of coefficient variation over time will be discussed. Third, the foundation for a more appropriate test of the input-output model will be examined. This will be followed by a concluding comment in Section 4.

1. THE STRUCTURE OF THE STATIC, OPEN INPUT-OUTPUT MODEL

In order to put the conventional tests of input-output analysis into perspective, the structure and the theoretical bases for these models will be summarized. Since the literature is replete with such discussions, this section will cover only a few selected areas.[1] This section begins with an exposition of the open, static input-output model and concludes with some remarks about its interpretation.

There are three assumptions which are typically made in input-output analysis. These are: (1) the economy can be divided into a finite number of sectors, each of which produces a single homogeneous product; (2) there are neither external economies nor diseconomies in production; and (3) the level of output in each sector uniquely determines the quantity of each input which is purchased.[2] This last assumption requires some further explanation as it has been given two distinct interpretations in the input-output literature. First, it could mean that all pairs of productive factors used in each sector are perfect complements. In other words, changes in relative prices have no effect on factor proportions. Second, the statement is actually true if the economic system is competitive and if there is but one scarce factor of production. In this case, there is only one thing on which to economize and, as a consequence, relative price changes would not be possible.[3]

In any case, these three assumptions imply that the production function for the jth sector may be expressed as

$$X'_j = \min\left[\frac{Z'_{1j}}{a'_{1j}}, \ldots, \frac{Z'_{mj}}{a'_{mj}}, \frac{Z'_{m+1,j}}{a'_{m+1,j}}, \frac{Z'_{m+2,j}}{a'_{m+2,j}}, \frac{V'_{1j}}{b'_{1j}}, \ldots, \frac{V'_{nj}}{b'_{nj}}\right] + \mu_j \qquad (2.1)$$

where

X'_j	= total quantity of output in sector j
Z'_{1j}	= total quantity of goods and services transferred from sector i to sector j, $i = 1, \ldots, m$
$Z'_{m+1,j}$	= total quantity of a homogeneous labor service purchased by sector j from sector i
$Z'_{m+2,j}$	= total quantity of a homogeneous public service purchased by sector j from governmental agencies
V'_{ij}	= total quantity of various types of inputs purchased by sector j from outside the geographic boundaries of the economy in question, $i = 1, \ldots, n$
a'_{ij}	= technical coefficient interpreted as the minimum quantity of output from sector i required to produce one unit of output in sector j; where $a'_{ij} > 0, i = 1, \ldots, m + 2, j = 1, \ldots, m$
b'_{ij}	= trade coefficient interpreted as the minimum quantity of import i required to produce one unit of output in sector j, $b'_{ij} > 0, i = 1, \ldots, n, j = 1, \ldots, m$
$\min(a, b, \ldots, z)$	= minimum of the elements $(a, b, \ldots, z)$[4]
μ_j	= random disturbance term

It should be noted that production functions are generally not specified in stochastic form in input-output analysis. That is, input-output models are usually implemented as if they were deterministic. However, there are two important reasons why random disturbances should be explicitly included. First, these disturbances may arise from random measurement errors in the variables X'_j, Z'_{ij}, or V'_{ij}.[5] Second, variables affecting X'_j may have been omitted from the argument list in equation (2.1). Examples of such variables might include the vintage and condition of capital; entrepreneurial effort and luck; and, in the case of agricultural sectors, weather.

From equation (2.1) estimates of the technical coefficients may be obtained from a relation of the form

$$Z'_{ij} = a'_{ij}X'_j + \theta'_{ij} \tag{2.2}$$

where $\theta'_{ij} = a'_{ij}\mu_j$. In addition, the trade coefficients are estimable from

$$V'_{ij} = b'_{ij}X'_j + \pi'_{ij} \tag{2.3}$$

where $\pi'_{ij} = b'_{ij}\mu_j$. However, data on Z'_{ij}, V'_{ij} and X'_j have seldom been available to input-output analysts. As a result, in empirical interindustry models, these variables are usually redefined as their value counterparts which implies

$$Z_{ij} = a_{ij}X_j + \theta_{ij} \tag{2.4}$$

$$V_{ij} = b_{ij}X_j + \pi_{ij} \tag{2.5}$$

where Z_{ij} is the value of goods and services transferred from i to j, V_{ij} is the value of the ith import purchased by j, X_j is the total value of output in j; a_{ij} and b_{ij}, which are still referred to as technical and trade coefficients, are interpreted as the minimum value of output in i required to produce one dollar's worth of output in j; and θ_{ij} and π_{ij} are understood to be appropriately redefined. Finally, because of the presumed deterministic nature of input-output models, the a_{ij} and b_{ij} are typically calculated by implicitly assuming that the error term is identically zero and forming the ratios, $a_{ij} = Z_{ij}/X_j$ and $b_{ij} = V_{ij}/X_j$.

In the remaining discussion, the estimation of trade coefficients will be ignored. This is not due to any presumption that this problem is unimportant in input-output analysis. To the contrary, in models of small, open regions, estimation of the trade coefficients is likely to be a matter of great concern. However, in the subsequent chapters, the reader will observe that the methods presented for estimating technical coefficients apply directly to the estimation of trade coefficients.

The ratio method described above for calculating the a_{ij} has been criticized by several authors.[6] Essentially, they have observed, if these coefficients are calculated according to $a_{ij} = Z_{ij}/X_j$, the resulting input-output model appears to be deterministic because only one observation can be obtained from a set of cross-sectional data. In particular, Klein has argued that such an estimation procedure has undesirable features from a statistical point of view.

The ease with which the structural parameters ... a_{ij} ... can be estimated, given the data on ... (total outputs and flows between sectors) is deceptive. The model is assumed to consist of a series of one parameter production functions, and one observation is used to estimate the single parameter. In a statistical sense there are no degrees of freedom and we have no idea about the reliability or probabilistic properties of the estimated parameters.[7]

This lack of attention to statistical problems has led input-output analysts to weak and inconclusive tests of their models. The following review of the literature will provide evidence for this view.

2. TESTS OF TECHNICAL COEFFICIENT VARIATION OVER TIME

As the literature attests, a great number of researchers have sought to test the workability of input-output analysis.[8] As noted previously, most of these studies have concentrated on examining temporal variations in the technical coefficients. In this section, these investigations will be briefly, but critically, reviewed. The discussion is divided into two parts: (1) structural form tests of coefficient change, and (2) reduced from tests of coefficient change. In each part, the results of the leading studies will be presented.[9] This will be followed by some general criticisms to be levelled at their methodology.

A. Structural form tests

In one of the earliest studies, Cameron examined technical coefficient change in a one hundred seventy-eight sector model of the Australian economy over the period, 1935–1950.[10] So that his data would conform as nearly as possible with the assumptions of input-output analysis, he analyzed only the fifty-six sectors which met the following two conditions. First, sectoral output had to be approximately homogeneous both at a point in time and over time. Second, a time series of two observations had to be available on inputs and outputs in physical units. From these observations he calculated technical coefficients for the most important material inputs in each sector in order to determine the extent of their variation over time. Unfortunately, though, he reported only his results for ten sectors. These have been summarized by Chenery and Clark in the table which is reproduced below.[11] On the whole, Cameron concluded, the technical coefficients under examination showed substantial temporal stability.

Obviously, Cameron's conclusion might have been quite different had he included all sectors in his analysis. In fact, much of the later research on coefficient variation has focused on the two problems which he chose not

Table 2.1. Results of Cameron's study of technical coefficient variation between 1935–50.

Range of percentage mean deviation*	Number of coefficients
0–2%	12
2–4%	13
4–6%	3
6–8%	3
8–10%	1
10–12%	1
	33

*Percentage mean deviations were determined by taking the average coefficient deviation from the mean as a percentage of the mean.

to consider; sectors which have heterogeneous outputs and sectors for which data on inputs and outputs are unavailable in physical units. There are important reasons why such investigations can be justified. For example, in a practical setting the assumption of homogeneous products for each sector is, to some extent, always violated. As a result, technical coefficients may change over time due to variations in product mix. Also, if only data on value of transactions are available, conversion to physical units may be difficult if these transactions did not occur at a single price. As has been widely recognized, these two problems are potential sources of coefficient instability.

In a representative study which sought to investigate these problems, Sevaldson examined the cork products sector of the Norwegian input-output accounts.[12] To this effect, he gathered annual data on the value of inputs and outputs for the thirteen firms which operated over the period 1949–1954. From these data, he calculated both the value technical coefficient for raw cork and its volume counterpart. As its name suggests, the value coefficients were obtained from the original data. On the other hand, the volume coefficients were derived by first deflating the appropriate observations to 1950 monetary units. Although the firms in this sector produced a diversified range of products, both types of coefficients exhibited temporal stability. However, as Table 2.2 indicates, the volume coefficients exhibited far less variability.[13]

The preceding study can be criticized because only two sectors were considered (see footnote 12). In the mid 1960's, then, further research was undertaken in order to consider the questions which Sevaldson raised. Tilanus conducted an investigation which at least partially filled this gap.[14] He examined the temporal stability of value coefficients in each sector of the Dutch input-output tables over the period 1948–1961. Since these

Table 2.2.   Sevaldson's calculations of the raw cork input coefficient for the cork products sector 1949–1954.

	1949	1950	1951	1952	1953	1954	Average	Standard deviation
Value	44.0	51.4	57.4	54.7	51.7	57.5	52.8	4.6
Volume	49.6	51.3	51.7	51.8	49.9	51.7	51.0	0.9

tables contained only thirty-five sectors, the output of each sector was quite heterogeneous. Contrary to Sevaldson, Tilanus found evidence of large temporal variations for these coefficients. In fact, about 40% of the coefficients which he considered exhibited strong loglinear trends. It is significant that these findings were especially true for the less important inputs which Sevaldson did not consider.

Finally, the most imaginative test of coefficient variation over time was conducted by Tilanus and Theil.[15] They noted that since each sector's production function is assumed to exhibit constant returns to scale, then $\sum_{i=1}^{m} a_{ij} + \sum_{i=1}^{n} b_{ij} = 1$. Furthermore, since these $m + n$ fractions are non-negative, they can be regarded as a set of probabilities. As the authors suggested, this fact makes it possible to use information theory to evaluate forecasts of input coefficients. To demonstrate this proposition, let

$$a_j(t) = \{a_{1j}(t), a_{2j}(t), \ldots, a_{mj}(t), b_{.j}(t)\} \tag{2.6}$$

where $b_j = \sum_{i=1}^{n} b_{ij}$ be a set of calculated technical coefficients for the jth sector in the year t. Under the assumption that these parameters are constant over time, this set constitutes a forecast of its counterpart in the year $t + s$. Next, form the following index for the accuracy of this forecast

$$I(a_j(t + s) : a_j(t)) = \sum_i a_{ij}(t + s) \log \frac{a_{ij}(t + s)}{a_{ij}(t)} \tag{2.7}$$

As can easily be verified, $I(\cdot) = 0$ if $a_{ij}(t + s) = a_{ij}(t)$ for $i = 1, \ldots m$. Otherwise, the index is always positive and its magnitude depends upon the disparity between $a_j(t)$ and $a_j(t + s)$.

Tilanus and Theil used this approach to analyze a time series of ten observations on the largest four value technical coefficients for each of fifteen sectors (out of a possible thirty-five) in the Dutch input-output tables over the period 1948–1957. Essentially, they found a considerable and continuous drift of the input structure over time. That is, as s increased, the index in (2.7) rose substantially for nearly all sectors. As they pointed out, though, the rate of increase for the index tended to decrease with increases in s.

Actually, the studies just reviewed have produced but one rather unpromising conclusion. In particular, due to such problems as product heterogeneity and price changes, technical coefficients vary over time. But is this variability 'high' or 'low'? That is, do these studies provide evidence which can be used to reject a statistical hypothesis of temporal invariance? From a deterministic point of view, the answer is trivially affirmative. However, in a probabilistic sense, the answer should be emphatically no!

The reason why this is true lies in the method used to estimate the technical coefficients. As was indicated previously, if the technical coefficients are calculated according to $a_{ij} = Z_{ij}/X_j$, then standard errors for these estimates cannot be obtained from cross-sectional data. However, it is easy to imagine that a time series of these coefficients may be a set of random drawings from a common parent population. Consequently, since no allowance has been made for such stochastic variation, there is no way to judge which coefficient changes are significant and which are not.

This weakness in the study of temporal coefficient variability has had a serious methodological side-effect. Specifically, it has made input-output one of the leading tools used to study structural change in economic systems.[16] Such an observation should hardly come as a surprise because it was predicted by Rasmussen nearly twenty years ago. He stated, '. . . it is quite clear that *a priori*, it would be most surprising if an application of the model would not make it inevitable to make extensive use of "structural changes" as an "explanation" of the . . . deviations between the predictions of the model and actual observations.'[17] The explanation for this is straightforward. Since there has been no allowance for random coefficient variation, any fluctuations which are worth mentioning can be attributed to structural change.

B. *Reduced form tests*

The reduced form forecasting tests represent a second class of techniques which have been used to evaluate temporal stability of input-output coefficients. These tests are somewhat more interesting than the ones just reviewed because they examine the viability of the model in a particularly attractive application. That is, they show how well input-output models predict an economy's total output vector at a future point in time.

Although these forecasts may turn out to be inaccurate, they are quite simple to obtain. Once values for the technical coefficients have been calculated, forecasts may be obtained from equation (1.2), which is reproduced below as equation (2.8). This is

$$X(t + s) = (I - A)^{-1} Y(t + s) \tag{2.8}$$

where the mxm matrix $(I - A)^{-1}$ is often called the Leontief inverse. Then, if the vector of final demands (Y) is known for some future time, a forecast for X can be easily determined on the assumption that A is constant over time. Obviously, if these two conditions hold exactly, then the vector of total outputs would be predicted without error. But as the evidence in the preceding section demonstrates, the elements of A often change substantially over time. In addition, final demand is often difficult to define; much less predict. The purpose of the reduced form tests, then, is to determine the effect of these two problems on forecasts of the vector of total outputs.

It should be emphasized at the outset that the reduced form tests suffer from the same weakness as those which were summarized in the previous section.[18] Because no allowance has been made for stochastic variation in A, it is not possible to compute standard errors and confidence intervals for X. In order to circumvent this problem, many of the reduced form investigations have been comparison tests. In other words, these studies tried to determine if input-output forecasts are more accurate than other (arbitrarily chosen) predictive techniques.

There are three techniques which have often been compared with input-output as a forecasting tool. The first is GNP extrapolation. Here, the output of each sector is hypothesized to grow at the same rate as GNP. Predicted output in the jth sector for the year $t + s$ given an observation for output in the year t, then, is

$$X_j^p(t + s) = \frac{\text{GNP} \, (t + s)}{\text{GNP} \, (t)} X_j(t) \qquad (2.9)$$

Final demand extrapolation is a second and similar technique. Using this method, the output of each sector is projected to grow at a rate which is proportional to its own final demand. Thus, for any sector, predicted output is

$$X_j^p(t + s) = \frac{Y_j(t + s)}{Y_j(t)} X_j(t) \qquad (2.10)$$

Third, and finally, a multiple regression technique has been used. That is, predicted outputs are simply extrapolations from an estimated equation of the form

$$X_j^p(t) = \beta_0 + \beta_1 \, \text{GNP} \, (t) + \beta_2 t + \mu(t) \qquad (2.11)$$

These comparative studies have been conducted on widely differing sets of data. Even so, their results generally rank the four techniques according to predictive accuracy as (1) multiple regression, (2) input-output, (3) final demand extrapolation, and (4) GNP extrapolation. This conclusion is illustrated in the comparative tests of Barnett and is, at least, not contradicted by a similar study by Adams and Stewart. Both of these investigations will be considered in turn.

Barnett began by taking the input-output forecasts of total output in twenty-eight sectors of the United States' economy for 1950 which were compiled by Cornfield, Evans, and Hoffenberg.[19] These forecasts were obtained from (2.8) using Leontief's 1939 estimates of the production coefficients and a final demand vector which was projected in 1947. The input-output predictions were then compared with those of the other three techniques. Table 2.3 shows the results.[20]

From the point of view of input-output forecasting, the evidence provided in Table 2.3 is at least mildly distressing. The multiple regression method not only seems to work better, it is less expensive to use. In addition, confidence limits can be attached to the multiple regression predictions. As was indicated earlier, this information cannot be obtained for input-output forecasts.

In a second and later study, Adams and Stewart conducted an investigation which was in much the same spirit as Barnett's.[21] However, there were two methodological differences. First, Adams and Stewart did not construct multiple regression forecasts. Second, final demand vectors were taken as given data since these authors made backward projections or backcasts. In particular, they employed the 1935 input-output table for

Table 2.3. Results of Barnett's comparative study of four forecasting techniques.

Forecasting method	Weighted mean percentage error*
Multiple regression**	22%
Input-output	29%
Final demand extrapolation	32%
GNP extrapolation	36%

*These were calculated by

$$\sum_{j=1}^{28} \frac{X_j^p(t+s) - X_j(t+s)}{\sum_{k=1}^{28} X_k(t)}$$

where $X_j(\cdot)$ = actual output in sector j, $X_j^p(\cdot)$ = predicted output in sector j, $t = 1939$, $t + s = 1950$.
**Estimates of the parameters in (2.11) were obtained by using the time series of annual data; 1922–1941 and 1946.

Table 2.4. Comparison of errors in output projections by Adams and Stewart.

Projection by percent error	I–O	1924 Final demand extrapolation	GNP Extra-polation	I–O	1930 Final demand extrapolation	GNP Extra-polation
0–5	30	9	18	30	25	15
0–10	48	34	30	58	47	51
0–15	67	59	50	82	67	70
0–20	87	69	65	94	81	80
0–25	91	78	65	100	94	88
0–30	91	84	70	—	100	93
0–50	100	97	91	—	—	100
0–100	—	100	100	—	—	—

Great Britain and made backcasts for the total output of thirty-three sectors in both 1924 and 1930.

The discrepancies between actual and projected outputs, together with their counterparts for the final demand extrapolation and GNP extrapolation techniques are shown in Table 2.4 above.[22] As a matter of interpretation, the first entry in the first column of the table means that thirty percent of the backcasts for total sectoral output fell within five percent of the true value. Table 2.4, then, shows results which bear a close correspondence to those of Barnett. In particular, the projections of input-output appear to be more accurate than either of the two extrapolation techniques.

However, the Adams and Stewart study does not show input-output to be an unambiguously better predictive tool than the other two techniques. This is because they give input-output two hidden and possibly unfair advantages. First, there is no way to decide whether its superior forecasting accuracy (over, say, GNP extrapolation) is worth its extra cost. Second, input-output tables are so complicated to compile that they are often several years out of date by the time they are completed. Consequently, it may not be relevant to compare the predictions of the four techniques from the same base year. In other words, input-output projections (backcasts) from a particular year should be compared with those of other methods based on data from a later (earlier) period. Under these conditions, input-output forecasts might prove to be relatively less accurate.

The above discussion of the two comparative studies has probably been too harsh on input-output as a predictive tool. To set the record straight, it should be pointed out that several methods for updating technical coefficients have been designed to make input-output forecasts more accurate. For example, Stone has proposed the RAS method.[23] Essentially, this method embodies an hypothesis that, over time, these coefficients are subject to two effects: (1) an effect of fabrication and (2) an effect of substitution. According to Stone, the fabrication effect captures '... the extent to which commodity k has come to absorb a greater or smaller ratio of intermediate to primary inputs in its fabrication.'[24] Further, the substitution effect is '... measured by the extent to which the commodity; has been substituted for, or replaced by, other commodities as an intermediate input into industrial processes.'[25] Assuming that the effect of substitution on j is the same wherever j is used and fabrication changes in k uniformly affects all inputs used in making k, Stone was able to construct two mxm diagonal matrices of substitution and fabrication multipliers, R and S, such that $A^* = \text{RAS}$ where A^* is the matrix of updated coefficients. Even though the assumptions used in constructing A^* are quite strong, tests by Paelinck and Waelbroek showed that these new coefficients enabled predictions which were superior to the unadjusted input-output forecasts.[26]

3. STATISTICAL TESTS OF THE INPUT-OUTPUT MODEL

At this point, it should be apparent that the ideas of statistical theory have been virtually ignored in testing the usefulness of input-output analysis. However, there are a few exceptions to this statement as studies by Arrow and Hoffenberg, Quandt, and Long have focused on the application of probability theory to input-output analysis. The purpose of this section is to briefly review these results and to indicate their relationship to the material in the chapters to follow.

Arrow and Hoffenberg sought to test the hypothesis of temporal coefficient invariance.[27] As was the case in the studies just reviewed, they treated these coefficients as known constants at a point in time. Consequently, to investigate this hypothesis directly would have required a time series of input-output data. However, at the time of their writing, no such time series was available. As a result, they were forced to proceed indirectly. In particular, they took estimates of the technical coefficients which had been prepared for four sectors in the 1947 United States input-output tables. Next, they defined the constant coefficients prediction residual for each sector in the year $t + s$ to be

$$r_i(t + s) = X_i(t + s) - \sum_{j=1}^{m} a_{ij}(t) X_j(t + s) + Y_i(t + s) \qquad (2.12)$$

where the $a_{ij}(t)$ are the estimates of the technical coefficients for 1947, Y_i denotes final demand and $i = 1, \ldots 4$. Using equation (2.11) an annual time series was constructed for the prediction residuals over the period 1929–1950. Finally, the authors noted that if the temporal invariance hypothesis is valid, the $r_i(t + s)$ series should behave in a random fashion. On the other hand, if the converse is true, then $r_i(t + s)$ series should be functions of total outputs for each sector, final demands, and possibly other variables which are exogenous to the input-output model. In their empirical estimates, the converse was unmistakably supported. Specifically, several variables were found for each of the four sectors which explained a significant fraction of the variation in the constant coefficients prediction residuals.

Without doubt, the Arrow and Hoffenberg study provides the most conclusive evidence against the temporal invariance hypothesis. That is, these authors were able to reject this proposition even though they allowed for random fluctuations of the technical coefficients. However, their study has at least two shortcomings. First, using their approach, there is no way to study the variability of individual technical coefficients. Second, Arrow and Hoffenberg did not explicitly recognize that the technical coefficients might have random properties at a point in time.

Richard Quandt, though, has attempted to deal with both of these problems. In fact, he is one of the few economists who has recognized the need for studying the variance of the estimated technical coefficients at a point in time. His work has made two important contributions in this area. First, he showed how confidence intervals could be derived for the vector of total sectoral outputs in a reduced form system specified as equation (2.8).[28] In order to obtain this result, Quandt assumed that the observed matrix of technical coefficients was randomly drawn from a population of such matrices having a known probability distribution. By itself, this assumption is important because it takes account of the fact that input-output data are often obtained by sampling. Second, he demonstrated that the log-normal distribution is a useful approximation to the distribution of total sectoral outputs, regardless of the distribution of the technical coefficients.[29]

Although these results are quite interesting, they are of limited practical usefulness. This is because Quandt assumed knowledge of the probability distribution for the technical coefficients and, as a consequence, did not adequately treat the problem of estimating these parameters. In fact, in Quandt's only reference to the estimation problem, he stated, 'Since coefficients are to be obtained by sampling, it will be assumed that the means and variances of the input coefficients are known or can be closely approximated.'[30] Clearly, this statement over-simplifies the issue at hand: Once input-output relations are regarded as stochastic, there are many estimators which, in principle, may be used to obtain values for the technical coefficients.

To date, only one author, Wesley Long, appears to have dealt with the estimation of technical coefficients in a stochastic input-output model.[31]

Long's primary objective was to test the assumption of linear homogeneous production functions in input-output sectors and, therefore, his analysis bears on this subject only indirectly. Nevertheless, he suggested that regression may prove to be a useful tool in estimating the technical coefficients.[32] In fact, using data from the Philadelphia region, he estimated the parameters in equation (2.13) by ordinary least squares (OLS)

$$Z_{ij}^{(r)} = d_{ij} + a_{ij}X_j^{(r)} + u_{ij}^{(r)} \tag{2.13}$$

where the superscript refers to the rth firm in the jth sector, d_{ij} is a constant term and $u_{ij}^{(r)}$ a disturbance term. Obviously enough, if d_{ij} was constrained to equal zero, then (2.13) would produce estimates of Leontief-type technical coefficients.

There is no question that Long made a contribution toward resolving the estimation issue raised earlier. That is, if the technical coefficients are estimated by OLS, their standard errors may be easily calculated. However, this advantage is more apparent than real because, as will be argued in greater detail in Chapter 3, $X_j^{(r)}$ and $u_{ij}^{(r)}$ may not be independent. If this is the case, the OLS estimates of both a_{ij} and d_{ij} will be statistically biased and inconsistent.

4. CONCLUSION

This chapter has emphasized the need for obtaining measures of dispersion for a set of estimated technical coefficients. To date, such measures have not been developed and, as a consequence, tests of input-output analysis have produced few conclusive results. In fact, none of the tests described in this chapter are capable of discriminating between random temporal variations in the technical coefficients and structural change. Therefore, a great deal of work remains to be done in testing the effectiveness of input-output analysis in representing actual economic systems. In particular, a technique must be found which produces consistent estimates of both the technical coefficients and the standard errors for these estimates. Fortunately, these objectives are within reach if an appropriate regression method is used to estimate the technical coefficients. This application of regression to input-output models is discussed in Chapter 3.

NOTES

1. For more detailed treatments of the structure of input-output systems, see Otto Eckstein, 'The Input-Output System – Its Nature and Use,' *Economic Activity Analysis*, ed. Oskar Morganstern, New York, John Wiley and Sons, 1954, pp. 43–78; Robert Dorfman, Paul

A. Samuelson and Robert M. Solow, *Linear Programming and Economic Analysis*, New York, McGraw-Hill, 1958; and William H. Miernyk, *The Elements of Input-Output Analysis*, New York, Random House, 1965.

2. Hollis B. Chenery and Paul G. Clark, *Interindustry Economics*, New York, John Wiley and Sons, 1959, pp. 33–42.

3. On this point, see Paul A. Samuelson, 'Abstract of a Theorem Concerning Substitution in Open Leontief Systems,' *Activity Analysis of Production and Allocation*, ed. Tjalling Koopmans, New York, John Wiley and Sons, 1951; and Sanjit Bose, 'A New Proof of the Non-Substitution Theorem,' *International Economic Review*, XIII, February, 1972.

4. Robert Dorfman, Paul A. Samuelson, and Robert M. Solow, *Linear Programming and Economic Analysis*, New York, McGraw-Hill, 1958, p. 231. Also note that if all inputs are perfectly divisible and if there is no waste, the minimum of the elements $(a, b, ..., z)$ will equal the maximum.

5. The issue of measurement errors in an input-output setting has been previously discussed by two authors. C. B. Tilanus, *Input-Output Experiments: The Netherlands, 1948–1961*, Rotterdam, *Rotterdam University Press*, 1966. Michael Bacharach, *Biproportional Matrices and Input-Output Change*, Cambridge, Cambridge University Press, 1970.

6. See also P. N. Rasmussen, *Studies in Intersectoral Relations*, Amsterdam, North-Holland, 1956, pp. 45–47; and Leonid Hurwicz, 'Input-Output Analysis and Economic Structure,' *American Economic Review*, XLV, September, 1955, 631.

7. Lawrence Klein, *A Textbook of Econometrics*, Englewood Cliffs, N.J., Prentice-Hall, 1974, pp. 341–42.

8. For a recent review of this literature, see Bacharach, *Biproportional Matrices and Input-Output Change*, pp. 10–16.

9. Often, these studies will appear to be somewhat dated. However, the more recent efforts, which will be indicated in the bibliography, typically obtain the same or similar results. In addition, they are usually less comprehensive.

10. Burgess Cameron, 'The Production Function in Leontief Models,' *The Review of Economic Studies*, XX(1), 1952–1953.

11. Chenery and Clark, *Interindustry Economics*, p. 164.

12. Per Sevaldson, 'Changes in Input-Output Coefficients,' *Structural Interdependence and Economic Development*, ed. Tibor Barna, New York, St. Martin's Press, 1963. Sevaldson also examined the wood products sector. His results are not reproduced here as they are much the same as for the cork products sector.

13. *Ibid.*, p. 315.

14. C. B. Tilanus, *Input-Output Experiments: The Netherlands 1948–1961*, Rotterdam, Rotterdam University Press, 1966, pp. 36–51.

15. C. B. Tilanus and Henri Theil, 'The Information Approach to the Evaluation of Input-Output Forecasts,' *Econometrica*, XXXII, October, 1965.

16. For example, see Ann P. Carter, *Structural Change in the American Economy*, Cambridge, Mass., Harvard University Press, 1970.

17. Rasmussen, *Studies in Intersectoral Relations*, p. 129.

18. An exception is Kenneth J. Arrow and Marvin M. Hoffenberg, *A Time Series Analysis of Interindustry Demands*, Amsterdam, North-Holland, 1959. This study will be reviewed in the final section.

19. Harold J. Barnett, 'Specific Industry Output Projections,' *Long Range Economic Projection*, ed. National Bureau of Economic Research, Princeton, Princeton University Press, 1954.

20. *Ibid.*, p. 202.

21. A. A. Adams and I. G. Stewart, 'Input-Output Analysis: An Application,' *The Economic Journal*, LXVI, September, 1956.

22. *Ibid.*, 451.

23. Other methods for updating matrices of technical coefficients have been proposed in Tilanus, *Input-Output Experiments: The Netherlands, 1948–1961* and in Bacharach, *Biproportional Matrices and Input-Output Change*. The interested reader may consult these books for a more thorough treatment of this topic.

24. Department of Applied Economics, University of Cambridge, 'Input-Output Relation-

ships 1954–1966,' *A Programme for Growth*, ed. Richard Stone, London, Chapman and Hall, 1963, p. 28.
25. *Ibid.*
26. Bacharach, *Biproportional Matrices*, pp. 27–30.
27. Arrow and Hoffenberg, *A Time Series of Interindustry Demands.*
28. Richard E. Quandt, 'On the Solution of Probabilistic Leontief Systems,' *Naval Research Logistics Quarterly*, VI, December, 1959. For another, and more recent, study in this vein, see Paul H. Tomlin, 'An Error Model for Projected Gross Outputs Using an Input-Output Table,' *Bureau of Census Research Memorandum* No. 212, 1973 and Paul H. Tomlin, 'Input-Output Error Analysis-Present Status,' *Bureau of Census Research Memorandum*, No. 317, 1973.
29. Richard E. Quandt, 'Probabilistic Errors in the Leontief System,' *Naval Research Logistics Quarterly*, V, July, 1958.
30. *Ibid.*, p. 159.
31. Wesley H. Long, 'An Examination of Linear Homogeneity of Trade and Production Functions in County Leontief Matrices,' *Journal of Regional Science*, IX, April, 1969, p. 47–69.
32. For a study which is similar to Long's; but which uses less complete data, see Iwao Ozaki, 'Economies of Scale and Input-Output Coefficients,' *Applications of Input-Output Analysis*, ed. A. P. Carter and A. Brody, Amsterdam, North-Holland, 1970, p. 280–302.

3. Input-output as a simple econometric model

The problem of calculating standard errors or other measures of dispersion for a set of estimated technical coefficients has been virtually ignored in input-output analysis. This omission represents a glaring weakness in studies of this type because the true technical coefficients cannot be known exactly. Although this point should be obvious, there are at least two reasons for this uncertainty which are worth mentioning. First, the data used to construct input-output models are often gathered by a non-exhaustive sampling of firms in each sector. Second, an observed matrix of technical coefficients obtained from census totals may still be a random drawing from a population of such matrices. This situation would arise, for example, if random measurement errors are present in the data. Therefore, without knowledge of the level of uncertainty associated with estimates of the technical coefficients, the value of input-output models for planning or forecasting purposes is unclear. This last point deserves special emphasis because empirical interindustry models are quite costly to construct.

The chapter to follow attempts to fill this gap in the input-output literature. In particular, the primary objective of this discussion is to show how two-stage least squares (TSLS) may be applied to cross-sectional data in order to obtain: (1) consistent estimates of the technical coefficients and (2) standard errors for these estimates.[1] The remainder of this chapter is organized into four sections. Section 1 recognizes the contributions of researchers who have recognized the problem of calculating standard errors for the technical coefficients. Some statistical properties of a ratio estimator are discussed in Section 2. Section 3, then, presents the TSLS technique which has both practical and theoretical advantages over the ratio method. Finally, an illustration of this simultaneous equation technique using cross-sectional data from West Virginia will be given in Section 4.

1. PRELIMINARIES

Even though comparatively little work has been devoted to the statistical properties of the technical coefficients, the calculation of a_{ij} according to $a_{ij} = Z_{ij}/X_j$ has been criticized by several authors. As was indicated in

Chapter 2, if these parameters are estimated in this way, the resulting input-output model is deterministic. This is because only one observation can be obtained on the ratio Z_{ij}/X_j from one set of cross-sectional data. In other words, after the technical coefficients have been determined there is no remaining information from which their standard errors may be calculated. This observation has stimulated a number of suggestions for calculating standard errors, which can be divided into two categories: (1) time series approaches and (2) cross-sectional approaches. In this section, each of these will be considered in turn.

A. Time series approaches

At first glance, there seems to be an easy way to solve the problem of estimating the technical coefficients together with their standard errors. That is, collect a time series on Z_{ij} and X_j and regress the former variable on the latter. But, in the past, this approach has not been used because data of this kind are almost always unavailable. Information regarding the Z_{ij} have proved to be especially elusive, particularly at the regional level.

However, due to the structure of the static, open input-output model, a time series on Z_{ij} is not really necessary. Specifically, it was pointed out in Chapter 1 that these models may be expressed as the set of m simultaneous equations shown in equation (1.1). This equation is reproduced below as equation (3.1).

$$X(t) = AX(t) + Y(t) \qquad\qquad (3.1)$$

Hence, if a sufficiently long time series on $X(t)$ and $Y(t)$ could be gathered, it might be feasible to estimate the m^2 parameters in (3.1) by regression.[2] However, when the number of sectors is of only moderate size (say, $m = 25$), a relatively long time series must be collected in order to estimate the elements of A.[3] Furthermore, even if enough data are available, structural change may render these estimates meaningless.[4]

B. Cross-sectional approaches

In addition to the time series approach, it is also possible to estimate the technical coefficients together with their standard errors from one set of cross-sectional data. Because it circumvents the problem of structural change and because its data requirements are drastically reduced, the cross-sectional approach has decided advantages over its time series counterpart. In fact, owing to these advantages, this approach will be considered exclusively throughout the remainder of this monograph. However, before it can be applied to estimation problems, an additional assumption must be clearly stated.

To implement the cross-sectional approach to estimating the technical coefficients, a new assumption is required which is typically not made in input-output analysis. In particular, all firms in each sector must have the same production function. Admittedly, this new assumption is a strong one. There is always the possibility that Leontief-type production functions provide an accurate description of sectors; but an inaccurate description of firms. However, as will be shown in the sections to follow, this assumption makes it feasible to calculate standard errors for the technical coefficients. Consequently, it should not be judged in terms of its lack of attention to reality. Instead, it ought to be judged according to the value of the results which it makes possible.

This additional assumption implies that the a_{ij} may be estimated according to the following modification of equation (2.4).

$$Z_{ij}^{(r)} = a_{ij}X_j^{(r)} + \theta_{ij}^{(r)} \tag{3.2}$$

where the superscript refers to the rth firm in the jth sector and where $\theta_{ij}^{(r)}$ is a disturbance term which is assumed to be independently and identically distributed (i.i.d.) with mean zero for all r.[5]

2. A RATIO ESTIMATOR FOR THE TECHNICAL COEFFICIENTS

In light of the above discussion, some statistical problems of a ratio estimator for the technical coefficients can be derived. This estimator, which is obtained by summing equation (3.2) over r and then dividing by $\sum_{r=1}^{n_j} X_j^{(r)}$, is given in equation (3.3).

$$\hat{a}_{ij}(R) = \sum_{r=1}^{n_j} Z_{ij}^{(r)} \left/ \sum_{r=1}^{n_j} X_j^{(r)} \right. \tag{3.3}$$

where n_j is the number of firms on which observations are taken. This estimator is thought to be interesting because it is identical to the standard ratio estimator Z_{ij}/X_j discussed in the first section of Chapter 2 on the condition that Z_{ij} is constructed from purchases data.[6] In this section it will be shown that $\hat{a}_{ij}(R)$ is biased and has a sampling variance which is difficult to estimate. To simplify matters, this argument is based on the assumption that each firm's inputs and outputs can be measured only with error. In other words, owing to factors such as slips of the pen in transcribing data, the measured values for $Z_{ij}^{(r)}$ and $X_j^{(r)}$ may not equal their true values.

This errors in variables assumption is made explicit in equation (3.4):

$$Z_{ij}^{(r)} = ZT_{ij}^{(r)} + u_{ij}^{(r)}$$
$$X_j^{(r)} = XT_j^{(r)} + w_j^{(r)} \tag{3.4}$$

In (3.4), $ZT_{ij}^{(r)}$ and $XT_j^{(r)}$ refer to the true, non-stochastic and unobservable intersectoral purchases and total output of the rth firm in sector j. On the other hand, $Z_{ij}^{(r)}$ and $X_j^{(r)}$ denote the measured or observable counterparts to $ZT_{ij}^{(r)}$ and $XT_j^{(r)}$, respectively. Finally, owing to these variable definitions, $u_{ij}^{(r)}$ and $w_j^{(r)}$ are measurement errors. For any i and j, these errors are assumed to be random and i.i.d. with zero mean for all r. In terms of equation (3.3), this specification implies that if $\theta_{ij}^{(r)}$ arises exclusively because of measurement errors

$$ZT_{ij}^{(r)} = a_{ij} XT_j^{(r)} \tag{3.5}$$

where

$$\theta_{ij}^{(r)} = u_{ij}^{(r)} - a_{ij} w_j^{(r)} \tag{3.6}$$

It was indicated by equation (3.3), $\hat{a}_{ij}(R)$ is just the measured total flow of goods and services from sector i to sector j divided by measured total output in sector j and is an estimator of a_{ij}. Due to equation (3.5), a_{ij} can be expressed as

$$a_{ij} = \sum_{r=1}^{n_j} ZT_{ij}^{(r)} \bigg/ \sum_{r=1}^{n_j} XT_j^{(r)} \tag{3.7}$$

To demonstrate the bias of the ratio estimator, rewrite equation (3.3) as

$$\hat{a}_{ij}(R) = \frac{\sum\limits_{r=1}^{n_j} ZT_{ij}^{(r)} + \sum\limits_{r=1}^{n_j} u_{ij}^{(r)}}{\sum\limits_{r=1}^{n_j} XT_j^{(r)} + \sum\limits_{r=1}^{n_j} w_j^{(r)}} \tag{3.8}$$

and put (3.8) in the form

$$\hat{a}_{ij}(R) = \frac{\sum\limits_{r=1}^{n_j} ZT_{ij}^{(r)}}{\sum\limits_{r=1}^{n_j} XT_j^{(r)}} + \frac{b}{c} = \frac{c \sum\limits_{r=1}^{n} ZT_{ij}^{(r)} + b \sum\limits_{r=1}^{n} XT_j^{(r)}}{c \sum\limits_{r=1}^{n_i} XT_j^{(r)}} \tag{3.9}$$

Since apart from a constant of proportionality,

$$\sum_{r=1}^{n_j} ZT_{ij}^{(r)} + \sum_{r=1}^{n_j} u_{ij}^{(r)} = c \sum_{r=1}^{n_j} ZT_{ij}^{(r)} + b \sum_{r=1}^{n_j} XT_j^{(r)}$$

$$\sum_{r=1}^{n_j} XT_j^{(r)} + \sum_{r=1}^{n_j} w_j^{(r)} = c \sum_{r=1}^{n_j} XT_j^{(r)} \tag{3.10}$$

it can be shown that

$$b = \frac{\displaystyle\sum_{r=1}^{n_j} u_{ij}^{(r)} - \left[\sum_{r=1}^{n_j} ZT_{ij}^{(r)} \sum_{r=1}^{n_j} w_j^{(r)} \bigg/ \sum_{r=1}^{n_j} XT_j^{(r)} \right]}{\displaystyle\sum_{r=1}^{n_j} XT_j^{(r)}}$$

$$\tag{3.11}$$

$$c = \frac{\displaystyle\sum_{r=1}^{n_j} XT_{ij}^{(r)} + \sum_{r=1}^{n_j} w_j^{(r)}}{\displaystyle\sum_{r=1}^{n_j} XT_j^{(r)}}$$

Hence, substituting (3.11) into (3.10) and using the definition in (3.7) yields

$$\hat{a}_{ij}(R) = a_{ij} + \frac{\displaystyle\sum_{r=1}^{n_j} u_{ij}^{(r)} - \left[\sum_{r=1}^{n_j} ZT_{ij}^{(r)} \sum_{r=1}^{n_j} w_j^{(r)} \bigg/ \sum_{r=1}^{n_j} XT_j^{(r)} \right]}{\displaystyle\sum_{r=1}^{n_j} XT_j^{(r)} + \sum_{r=1}^{n_j} w_j^{(r)}} \tag{3.12}$$

By inspection of (3.12) it should be apparent that the expected value of $\hat{a}_{ij}(R)$, is not, in general, equal to a_{ij}. In fact, this result holds even if the $u_{ij}^{(r)}$ are independent from the $w_j^{(r)}$. This is because the term $\sum_{r=1}^{n_j} ZT_{ij}^{(r)} \sum_{r=1}^{n_j} w_j^{(r)} / \sum_{r=1}^{n_j} XT_j^{(r)}$ in the numerator of (3.12) cannot be independent of the denominator. Therefore, the standard ratio estimator $\hat{a}_{ij}(R)$ is biased.

In defense of the ratio estimator, though, it should be pointed out that it is consistent.[7] To see this, let $\{\bar{u}_{ij}^{(r)}: r = 1,2 \ldots\}$ and $\{\bar{w}_j^{(r)}: r = 1, 2 \ldots\}$ be sequences of random variables where $\bar{u}_{ij}^{(r)} = \sum_{r=1}^{n_j} u_{ij}^{(r)}/n_j$ and $\bar{w}_j^{(r)} = \sum_{r=1}^{n_j} w_j^{(r)}/n_j$. Then by the assumptions in (3.4), both sequences converge to zero in quadratic mean as r approaches infinity.[8] As a result, by the properties of the plim operator it follows from equation (3.12) that

$$\plim_{n_j \to N_j} \hat{a}_{ij}(R) = a_{ij} \tag{3.13}$$

$$+ \frac{\plim_{n_j \to N_j} \left\{ \frac{1}{n_j} \sum_{r=1}^{n_j} u_{ij}^{(r)} - \left[\frac{1}{n_j^2} \sum_{r=1}^{n_j} ZT_{ij}^{(r)} \sum_{r=1}^{n_j} w_j^{(r)} \middle/ \frac{1}{n_j} \sum_{r=1}^{n_j} XT_j^{(r)} \right] \right\}}{\plim_{n_j \to N_j} \left\{ \frac{1}{n_j} \sum_{r=1}^{n_j} XT_j^{(r)} + \frac{1}{n_j} \sum_{r=1}^{n_j} w_j^{(r)} \right\}}$$

since

$$\lim_{n_j \to N_j} \frac{1}{n_j} \sum_{r=1}^{n_j} ZT_{ij}^{(r)}$$

and

$$\lim_{n_j \to N_j} \sum_{r=1}^{n_j} XT_{ij}^{(r)}$$

both converge to positive, finite constants for all i and j, the second term on the right hand side of (3.13) is equal to zero. Hence

$$\plim_{n_j \to N_j} \hat{a}_{ij}(R) = a_{ij}.$$

Equations (3.12) and (3.13) can also be used to show that the sampling variance of $\hat{a}_{ij}(R)$ is extremely complicated, even asymptotically. This point becomes obvious after expressing the asymptotic variance as

$$\plim_{n_j \to N_j} (\hat{a}_{ij}(R) - a_{ij})^2$$

$$= \plim_{n_j \to N_j} \left\{ \frac{\frac{1}{n_j} \sum_{r=1}^{n_j} u_{ij}^{(r)} - \left[\frac{1}{n_j^2} \sum_{r=1}^{n_j} ZT_{ij}^{(r)} \sum_{r=1}^{n_j} w_j^{(r)} \middle/ \frac{1}{n_j} \sum_{r=1}^{n_j} XT_j^{(r)} \right]}{\frac{1}{n_j} \sum_{r=1}^{n_j} XT_j^{(r)} + \frac{1}{n_j} \sum_{r=1}^{n_j} w_j^{(r)}} \right\}^2 \tag{3.14}$$

Consequently, there will be serious practical difficulties in obtaining an estimate for this measure.

3. REGRESSION ESTIMATES OF THE TECHNICAL COEFFICIENTS

As was indicated in the introduction, the technical coefficients may also be estimated by regression. In this section, two regression techniques will be considered; ordinary least squares (OLS) and TSLS. Basically, it will be argued that TSLS is superior to both OLS and to the ratio method.

It can be easily shown that estimating the technical coefficients by ordinary least squares leads to unpromising results.[9] To see why this is true, recall that the basic estimating equation is:

$$Z_{ij}^{(r)} = a_{ij}X_j^{(r)} + \theta_{ij}^{(r)} \tag{3.2}$$

Now, the effect of both error formats can be discussed. First, consider the errors in variables format where it has already been argued, using (3.4) that

$$\theta_{ij}^{(r)} = u_{ij}^{(r)} - a_{ij}w_j^{(r)} \tag{3.6}$$

Under this specification, equation (3.6) should be recognized as the classical errors in variables problem which is analyzed in many econometrics textbooks.[10] As is well-known, the OLS estimate of a_{ij} will be both biased and inconsistent.

Second, consider the errors in equations format. That is, assume the error term, $\theta_{ij}^{(r)}$, owes its existence to variables affecting $Z_{ij}^{(r)}$ which have been omitted from equation (3.2); rather than to imprecise measurements on $ZT_{ij}^{(r)}$ and $XT_j^{(r)}$. Next, note that from basic econometric theory, $X_j^{(r)}$ must be independent of $\theta_{ij}^{(r)}$ for OLS to yield unbiased estimates of the a_{ij}. But this condition is not likely to be satisfied because

$$X_j^{(r)} = \sum_{i=1}^{m} Z_{ij}^{(r)} + \sum_{i=1}^{n} V_{ij}^{(r)} \tag{3.15}$$

is an accounting identity which will be obeyed by any set of input-output data. This means that factors embodied in $\theta_{ij}^{(r)}$ which affect $Z_{ij}^{(r)}$ may be expected to affect $X_j^{(r)}$ as well. To illustrate this proposition, suppose that the rth firm in sector j experiences a random decrease in its effective capital stock due to unexpected equipment failures. In response, this firm might reduce purchases of other inputs, thus forcing a reduction in its level of output. Therefore, under the errors in equations format, OLS applied to (3.2) will result in biased and inconsistent estimates of the technical coefficients because, in general,

$$\operatorname*{plim}_{n_j \to N_j} (X_j^{(r)}\theta_j^{(r)}) \neq 0.$$

It is interesting to note that there is a common solution to the estimation problem under both error specifications. In particular, the a_{ij} can be consistently estimated if an appropriate instrument can be found to replace the explanatory variable. Fortunately, such instruments are not difficult to obtain if the matrix of technical coefficients is estimated column by column.

To be more specific, suppose that estimates for the a_{ij} are desired for the jth column. If this is the case, then, the set of equations to be estimated can be arranged much like a simple econometric model. An example of how this might be done is given in (3.16) below

$$X_j^{(r)} = \sum_{i=1}^{m} Z_{ij}^{(r)} + RV_j^{(r)} + WS_j^{(r)} + PG_j^{(r)}$$

$$Z_{1j}^{(r)} = a_{1j}X_j^{(r)} + \theta_{1j}^{(r)}$$

$$Z_{2j}^{(r)} = a_{2j}X_j^{(r)} + \theta_{2j}^{(r)}$$
$$\vdots$$
$$\tag{3.16}$$

$$Z_{mj}^{(r)} = a_{mj}X_j^{(r)} + \theta_{mj}^{(r)}$$

$$RV_j^{(r)} = a_{m+1,j}X_j^{(r)} + \theta_{m+1,j}^{(r)}$$

In the system of equations in (3.16), most of the relations need no further explanation as they are identical in form to (3.2). However, the first and last deserve some further comment. The first equation is an accounting identity stating that measured total output for any firm must be equal to its total payments to firms in the m endogenous sectors and to value added. As can be seen, value added has been broken down into three components. That is, $\sum_{i=1}^{n} V_{ij}^{(r)} = RV_j^{(r)} + WS_j^{(r)} + PG_j^{(r)}$.[11] The first, $RV_j^{(r)}$, represents that part of measured value added which is determined as a residual from $X_j^{(r)}$ and $Z_{ij}^{(r)}$. Clearly, items falling into this category, such as imports, profit, profits taxes, and gross receipts taxes, must be considered endogenous to the system in (3.16). On the other hand, the second component, $WS_j^{(r)}$, denotes wages and salaries; while a third, $PG_j^{(r)}$, represents payments to government such as property taxes. It is plausible to assume that these last two components can be measured without error and/or can be regarded as exogenous variables. This assumption can be justified on at least two grounds. First, firms are likely to keep accurate records of wage and salary and tax payments. This is especially true of wage and salary payments since this variable determines the employer Social Security contributions. Second, because contracting for labor services precedes product in any period and because of the types of tax payments included in $PG_j^{(r)}$, $WS_j^{(r)}$ and $PG_j^{(r)}$ may be treated as exogenous. Finally, the last equation in (3.16) is included because under the above decomposition in value added, $RV_j^{(r)}$ is an endogenous variable.

For identification of the kth equation ($k \geq 2$) in (3.16), the order condition requires that[12]

$$NP_k \geq NJ_k - 1 \tag{3.17}$$

In (3.17), NP_k denotes the number of predetermined variables in (3.16) which have been excluded from the kth equation while NJ_k denotes the number of jointly determined explanatory variables in equation k. This condition holds for each of the last $m + 1$ equations as $NP_k = 2$, ($WS_j^{(r)}$ and $PG_j^{(r)}$) while $NJ_k = 2$, ($Z_{ij}^{(r)}$ and $X_j^{(r)}$). Because of this result, it might appear as though each of these $m + 1$ equations is overidentified. However, the rank condition for identifiability requires that any *a priori* information regarding (3.16) be simultaneously imposed upon all equations. This condition implies that, for identification purposes, $WS_j^{(r)}$ and $PG_j^{(r)}$ must be treated as a single variable because they have been excluded from all equations to be estimated. In other words, $WS_j^{(r)}$ and $PG_j^{(r)}$ provide only one piece of information which can be used to distinguish between the equations in (3.16). Therefore, due to the rank condition, each of the last $m + 1$ equations in (3.16) is just-identified.

Because of the identification properties of the equations in (3.16), the a_{ij}; $i = 1, \ldots, m + 1$ may be estimated by TSLS. This, of course, amounts to using predicted values of the $X_j^{(r)}$ from the reduced form of (3.16) as instruments for the $X_j^{(r)}$ themselves. Estimating the technical coefficients in this way has at least three important advantages. First, as was indicated above, TSLS applied to (3.16) will produce consistent estimates of both the a_{ij} and the standard errors of these estimates. Second, it has the advantage of computational ease. Since there is only one explanatory variable (the jointly determined $X_j^{(r)}$) in each of the last $m + 1$ equations of (3.16), the TSLS estimator for the a_{ij} can be simplified as[13]

$$\hat{a}_{ij}(1) = \frac{X_j^T Q_j (Q_j^T Q_j)^{-1} Q_j^T Z_{ij}}{X_j^T Q_j (Q_j^T Q_j)^{-1} Q_j^T X_j} \tag{3.18}$$

where X_j and Z_{ij} are $n_j x 1$ vectors containing the $X_j^{(r)}$ and $Z_{ij}^{(r)}$ and where Q_j is an $n_j x 2$ matrix composed of the $WS_j^{(r)}$ and the $PG_j^{(r)}$. Furthermore, the asymptotic variance of the coefficient $\hat{a}_{ij}(1)$ may be calculated according to

$$\hat{\sigma}^2_{a_{ij}(1)} = \frac{\hat{\sigma}^2_{\theta ij}}{X_j^T Q_j (Q_j^T Q_j)^{-1} Q_j^T X_j} \tag{3.19}$$

Third, and perhaps most importantly, this approach casts the estimation of the technical coefficients in a traditional econometric setting. Once the problem is formulated as (3.16), the theory of estimating a system of simultaneous equations applies directly. This means, of course, that the choice of an estimator for the a_{ij} is very wide indeed. In addition to TSLS, any member of the k-class where plim $k = 1$ will provide consistent estimates of the technical coefficients.

IV. AN EXAMPLE OF THE TSLS TECHNIQUE USING DATA FROM WEST VIRGINIA

In the section below, the estimation of a set of technical coefficients by TSLS will be illustrated. Specifically, this estimation technique will be applied to input-output data from West Virginia obtained by Miernyk in 1965. This exercise is thought to be especially interesting since Miernyk's study of West Virginia is certainly one of the best regional input-output investigations conducted to date. The discussion will be divided into two parts: (1) a brief description of these data and (2) a presentation of empirical results.

A. Description of data

Using cross-sectional data for the year 1965, Miernyk and others constructed an input-output model of the state of West Virginia which was composed of the forty-eight endogenous sectors listed in column 2 of Table 3.1. As can be seen, this table also provides information on the total number of firms operating in each sector as of 1965 together with the Miernyk's sample sizes. These data indicate that Miernyk surveyed 406 firms; a sample which accounted for about 3.3% of the total number of firms operating in the state. With the aid of an interviewer, a representative of each firm completed an extensive questionnaire which called for information including an income statement and a detailed transactions summary.[14] These summaries showed each firm's in-state and out-of-state transactions (both purchases and sales) with economic units in each of the forty-eight sectors, with households, and with government at all levels. In addition, the purchases data indicated whether a particular expenditure was for raw materials or was a current expense. With Miernyk's cooperation, copies of the completed questionnaires from firms in thirty sectors were provided for use in the present study. These sectors, together with the number of usable questionnaires which were furnished are indicated in the fifth column of Table 3.1.[15]

Table 3.1.   West Virginia Input-Output Sectors for Which Data Were Furnished.

Sector number	Sector name	Number of firms in operation	Miernyk's sample size	Number of firms for which usable questionnaires were furnished
1	Agriculture	–	–	0
2	Coal mines (under ground)	1,311	8	4
3	Coal mines (strip and auger)	272	10	7
4	Petroleum and natural gas	305	4	0
5	All other mining	43	3	0
6	Building construction	556	8	7
7	Nonbuilding construction	288	5	5
8	Special trades construction	854	12	11
9	Food products (n.e.c.)	51	4	4
10	Food products (dairies)	38	3	6
11	Food products (bakeries)	40	6	0
12	Food products (beverages)	58	5	0
13	Apparel and accessories	37	4	0
14	Logging and sawmills	362	18	16
15	Furniture and wood fabrication	73	13	10
16	Printing and publishing	104	19	19
17	Chemicals	53	11	0
18	Petroleum	15	4	0
19	Glass	43	9	7
20	Stone and clay products	94	17	13
21	Primary metals	35	10	10
22	Fabricated metals	73	12	10
23	Machinery (except electrical)	98	10	8
24	Electrical machinery	18	5	4
25	Transportation equipment	11	3	0
26	Instruments and related products	10	3	0
27	All other manufacturing	69	14	7
28	Eating and drinking establishments	826	2	0
29	Wholesale trade	569	31	25
30	Retail food stores	442	3	0
31	Retail gasoline stations	226	9	9
32	All other retail	2,036	37	33
33	Banking	181	9	9
34	Other finance	187	3	0
35	Insurance agents and brokers	116	3	0
36	Real estate	193	9	7
37	All other FIRE	171	3	0
38	Hotels and lodgings	173	5	4
39	Medical and legal services	257	19	18
40	Educational services	22	3	0
41	All other services	1,354	14	11
42	Railroads	17	2	0
43	Trucking and warehousing	370	4	4
44	All other transportation	128	8	8
45	Communications	100	7	6
46	Electric companies and systems	21	7	0
47	Gas companies and services	31	7	6
48	Water and sanitary services	31	1	0

Source: Miernyk, *Simulating Regional Economic Development*, p. 10–15.

In order to estimate the technical coefficients according to the system of equations in (3.16), it was necessary to define each variable in terms of the entries on the questionnaire. These definitions, which are listed in Table 3.2, apply to the data collected from all firms in each sector. As a result, they are stated in terms of the rth firm in sector j.

Although most of the definitions provided in Table 3.2 are self-explanatory, there are three points which deserve some further comment. First, the customary distinction in input-output analysis between 'domestic' and 'foreign' intersectoral purchases has been observed: In-state purchases were included in $Z_{ij}^{(r)}$, while out-of-state purchases were placed in $RV_j^{(r)}$. Second, in-state raw materials purchases were adjusted for inventory changes to more accurately reflect the quantity which was actually used in production. Third, and finally, no use was made of the sales data which Miernyk collected. This is not because such information is of no value in estimating technical coefficients. To the contrary, it is possible to develop an analogue to (3.16) for estimating these parameters which uses sales data in place of purchases data. This discussion, however, is contained in Chapter 4.

Table 3.2. Definitions for the variables used in TSLS estimation of the technical coefficients.

Variable	Definition
$X_j^{(r)}$	total sales + ending inventories of goods in process and finished goods − beginning inventories of goods in process and finished goods.
$Z_{ij}^{(r)}$	purchases from in-state firms in sector i adjusted, in the case of raw materials purchases, for changes in raw materials inventory
$RV_j^{(r)}$	purchases from out-of-state firms + profits + profits taxes + gross receipts taxes + sales taxes + excise taxes
$WS_j^{(r)}$	payments to in-state and out-of-state households in the form of wages and salaries + supplements to wages
$PG_j^{(r)}$	licenses and fees + property tax payments to in-state and out-of-state local and state governments + any remaining payments to the federal government

B. Presentation of empirical results

Since the West Virginia model contained forty-eight endogenous sectors, there were, at most, forty-eight technical coefficients to estimate in each of the twenty-nine sectors for which usable data were provided. Conse-

Table 3.3.   TSLS estimates of four technical coefficients from Sector 3.

Coefficient number	TSLS	GQ	TSLS$_H$	GQ$_H$
5	.30963–04	+	.41340–04	–
	(.35322–04)		(.50949–04)	
29	.97548–01**	–		
	(.12401–01)			
36	.66602–01**	–		
	(.74930–02)			
46	.20406–02**	+	.18313–02	–
	(.42905–03)		(.84400–03)	

(1) Standard errors given in parentheses
(2) **denotes significance at 1% level using a t-test with 6 degrees of freedom
(3) *denotes significance at 5% level under same test
(4) + denotes presence of heteroskedasticity under Goldfeld–Quandt test at 1% level.
(5) – denotes absence of same.

quently, this sub-section will be confined to presenting an example of the estimation procedure and to discussing the empirical results in general terms.[16]

To illustrate the TSLS estimation of the technical coefficients in equation (3.16), consider the subset of results which are presented in Table 3.3. The extreme left-hand column of Table 3.3 indicates the 'row number' of the technical coefficient under consideration.[17] These 'row numbers,' it should be noted, are drawn from Table 3.1. As a result, the values in, say, the second line on Table 3.3 pertain to the parameter $a_{29,3}$; the minimum value of wholesale trade required to produce one dollar's worth of output from the strip and auger coal mining sector.

In the second column of Table 3.3, TSLS estimates of the four technical coefficients are presented together with their respective standard errors. These results indicate that Coefficients 29, 36, and 46 are different from zero at the 1% level of significance.[18] On the other hand, the estimate for Coefficient 5 is not significant at the 5% level.

Next, Column 3 shows that heteroskedasticity, an econometric problem which may cause inaccurate estimates of the coefficient standard errors, was likely to be present in estimating two of the four coefficients under consideration in Table 3.3. Specifically, a '+' or '–' in this column indicates its probable presence or absence. In order to arrive at this conclusion, it was conjectured that the variance of the error term in the estimating equation for each of the four coefficients was proportional to the square of $WS_j^{(r)}$.[19] Then, this sector's seven observations were arranged in descending order according to this variable and the Goldfeld-Quandt test was performed at the 1% level of significance.[20]

Finally, Columns 4 and 5 provide the results from re-estimating Coefficients 5 and 46 to take account of the heteroskedasticity problem. These values were obtained by dividing each variable in (3.16) by $WS_j^{(r)}$ and running TSLS on the transformed system of equations. As can be seen from Column 5, this operation was successful in reducing heteroskedasticity according to the Goldfeld-Quandt test. However, Column 4 indicates that the significance of Coefficient 46 was destroyed at the five percent level.

The empirical estimates presented in Table 3.3 are not meant to be representative of the results for all twenty-nine sectors. Consequently, this larger body of estimates should also be summarized. In doing so, attention will be focused on the number of coefficient estimates which are significantly different from zero at the 5% level of significance. Table 3.4 presents these results.

In Table 3.4, Column 2 indicates the number of estimating equations in each of the twenty-nine sectors for which at least one observation on the dependent variable was positive. Obviously enough, no calculation was required to show that the coefficient estimates in the remaining equations were identically equal to zero. The third and fifth columns, then, present the number of significant coefficients for each sector before and after transforming the data where necessary to account for heteroskedasticity. The number of heteroskedasticity transformations for each sector is given in Column 4.

An examination of Column 4 of Table 3.4 reveals that the severity of the heteroskedasticity problem varied greatly between sectors. For example, nearly all the estimating equations for Sectors 2, 8, and 14 required transformation to deal with this problem. On the other hand, no heteroskedasticity transformations were required for Sectors 9, 19, 24, 38, and 43. As might be expected from past econometric work, the sectors where the heteroskedasticity problem was most severe generally suffered the greatest loss of significant coefficients. Table 3.4 shows that at the 5% level, Sector 2 lost 14 significant coefficients while Sector 14 lost 6. However, for the 29 sectors taken together, only 31 coefficients turned insignificant.

Table 3.4 also indicates that after adjusting for heteroskedasticity, 255 coefficients estimates are significant at the 5% level. This represents about 36.4% of the 701 coefficients estimated. Alternatively stated, of the total number of possible coefficient estimates in these 29 sectors of the West Virginia model ($48 \times 29 = 1392$), 1137 or 81.7% were either not significantly different from zero or identically equal to zero. These results should not be taken as an indictment of the West Virginia model. Instead, it should be stressed that this chapter made use of data from only 29 of the possible 48 sectors. Furthermore, the sales data which Miernyk collected were not

Table 3.4. Statistically significant coefficients under TSLS estimation at 5% level.

Sector	Number of coefficients estimated	Number significant before adjustment	Number of adjustments	Number significant after adjustment
2	23	18	21	4
3	24	15	5	14
6	22	11	1	11
7	32	16	0	16
8	24	10	19	6
9	22	6	0	6
11	21	10	8	4
14	29	12	22	6
15	25	12	7	11
16	25	18	11	17
19	20	8	0	8
20	30	11	4	11
21	30	6	6	5
22	30	10	14	9
23	25	10	3	8
24	20	1	0	1
27	24	4	4	4
29	34	12	15	13
31	18	7	5	8
32	39	20	22	17
33	21	13	5	10
36	21	15	3	15
38	17	8	0	8
39	28	13	13	13
41	24	6	6	6
43	19	5	0	5
44	21	3	4	2
45	13	2	3	1
47	20	20	6	16
Total	701	302	207	255

employed in the estimation process. However, this last deficiency can be remedied as it is possible to modify the system of equations in (3.16) in order that sales, rather than purchases, data are required. This modification is described in Chapter 4 in connection with the reconciliation problem.

NOTES

1. The term 'consistency' has been given a great many interpretations in input-output analysis. Under one interpretation, it means that the accounts for all productive units in an economic system are balanced. For a description of other interpretations, see Richard Stone, 'Consistent Projections in Multi-Sector Models,' *Activity Analysis in the Theory of Growth and Planning*, ed. E. Malinvaud and M. O. L. Bacharach, New York, St. Martin's Press, 1967, pp. 232–44. It must be emphasized, though, that none of these definitions are relevant in this discussion. Here, and in what follows, 'consistency' means consistency in a statistical sense.

2. This suggestion is due to Lawrence Klein, *A Textbook of Econometrics*, Englewood Cliffs, New Jersey, Prentice-Hall, 1974, p. 344.
3. Briggs encountered this very problem in F. E. A. Briggs, 'On Problems of Estimation in Leontief Models,' *Econometrica*, XXV, July, 1957. Since the author had a time series of only six observations, he was forced to proceed at an extremely high level of aggregation.
4. For a discussion of the importance of structural change in an input-output context, see Ann Carter, *Structural Change in the American Economy*, Cambridge, Mass., Harvard University Press, 1970.
5. It might be noted that since $Z_{ij}^{(r)}$ denotes purchases by the rth firm in sector j from all firms in sector i, equation (3.2) will produce 'columns only' estimates of a_{ij}. 'Rows only' estimates will be discussed in Chapter 4.
6. For a case where Z_{ij} was actually constructed in this way, see Walter Isard and Thomas Langford, *Regional Input-Output Study: Recollections, Reflections, and Diverse Notes on the Philadelphia Experience*, Cambridge, Mass., MIT Press, 1971.
7. It should be noted that in theory, asymptotic distributions are obtained by making the sample size arbitrarily large. However, in the present case, the sample size in sector j, n_j, can only be as large as N_j, the total number of firms in that sector. This proviso should be kept in mind throughout the remainder of this monograph.
8. Phoebus J. Dhrymes, *Econometrics: Statistical Foundations and Applications*, New York, Harper and Row, 1970, p. 90.
9. It might be recalled from Chapter 2, p. 17, that OLS was suggested as a desirable technique for estimating technical coefficients by Wesley H. Long, 'An Examination of Linear Homogeneity of Trade and Production Functions in County Leontief Matrices,' *Journal of Regional Science*, IX, April, 1969.
10. For example, see J. Johnston, *Econometric Methods*, New York, McGraw-Hill, 1972, p. 281–91.
11. This specification is clearly arbitrary as there are numerous other ways of separating the components of value added. However, the above decomposition is intended only as an illustration.
12. See Franklin M. Fisher, *The Identification Problem in Econometrics*, New York, McGraw-Hill, 1966, pp. 39–45 for a more complete treatment of the identification problem.
13. Dhrymes, *Econometrics*, p. 187. In addition, the notation for the TSLS estimate of a_{ij}, $\hat{a}_{ij}$ (1), derives from the fact that TSLS is a member of the k-class with $k = 1$.
14. This questionnaire is reproduced in William Miernyk, *et al.*, *Simulating Regional Economic Development*, Lexington, Mass., D. C. Heath, 1970, pp. 208–220.
15. As might be expected, many of the questionnaires provided were in poor condition. For example, some of them did not contain income statements and the transactions summaries given on others were little more than guesswork. As a result, some of the questionnaires which Miernyk provided were disregarded in the present study. In fact, none of the questionnaires from Sector 17 (chemicals) were used. A more complete discussion of these and other problems with the West Virginia data is available from the author on request.
16. For the reader who is interested in the results for individual coefficients, TSLS estimates are provided for sectors 14, 16, 20, 29, 32 in Appendix 4.A. To interpret the entries in Appendix 4.A, it should be observed that only 'columns only' estimates are discussed in this chapter, while a corresponding 'rows only' estimator is developed in Chapter 5. Finally, a more complete set of 'columns only' estimates constructed by TSLS is available from the author upon request.
17. For Miernyk's own estimates of these coefficients, see Miernyk, *et al.*, *Simulating Regional Economic Development*, pp. 246–47. It should be noted, though, that there is no way to make comparisons between Miernyk's coefficient estimates and those reported here. This is largely because Miernyk's reported coefficients were calculated with the aid of the sales data referred to earlier.
18. In order to perform coefficient significance tests, the statistic $\hat{a}_{ij}/\hat{\sigma}_{a_{ij}}$ was assumed to be t-distributed with $n_j - 1$ degrees of freedom. Although this procedure has no theoretical foundation, it is recommended on the basis of Monte Carlo evidence in R. Jeffery Green, 'Alternative Significance Tests for TSLS Estimated Parameters: Some Monte Carlo Evidence, *Metroeconomica*, XXV, May–August, 1973, p. 193.

19. If this were a single equation setting, it might be more natural to assume the variance of the error term to be proportional to the square of $X_j^{(r)}$. However, such an assumption in case at hand would only create other serious problems. It implies, for example, that to take account of heteroskedasticity, all the variables in system (3.16) should be divided by $X_j^{(r)}$. However, this operation would leave only one exogenous variable in the system; a vector of units. The present assumption, that $E(\theta_{ij}^{(r)2} = \lambda(X_j^{(r)2})$ for constant λ does not strain credibility, though, because for Sector 3, the correlation between $X_j^{(r)}$ and $WS_j^{(r)}$ was .928.
20. Steven M. Goldfeld and Richard E. Quandt, 'Some Tests for Homoskedasticity,' *Journal of the American Statistical Association*, LX, September, 1965, p. 540–41.

4. On the use of the variance in resolving two practical problems often encountered in input-output analysis

The preceding chapter provided an exposition of the TSLS method of estimating a set of technical coefficients. It was argued that TSLS produces both consistent estimates of these parameters and consistent estimates of the coefficient standard errors. These standard errors were interpreted as measures of the uncertainty associated with observing the true technical coefficients. In the discussion to follow, this interpretation of the TSLS standard errors will be applied in dealing with two problems which are often encountered in regional input-output analysis. These problems are: (1) reconciling 'rows only' and 'columns only' estimates of the technical coefficients and (2) choosing sectoral sample sizes for purposes of data collection.

The purpose of this chapter is to recommend improved techniques for handling the problems of reconciliation and sample size selection. These recommendations, which are natural extensions of the results in Chapter 3, are based on the principle of minimum variance. Specifically, with regard to the problem of reconciling 'rows only' and 'columns only' estimates, the following two-step procedure is suggested: First, use TSLS to calculate both types of estimates for each technical coefficient; and second, apply the standard theorems on linear combinations of random variables in order to find the minimum variance reconciled estimator. Section 1 will develop this procedure in greater detail and provide an illustration using the West Virginia data described in Chapter 3. Section 2, then, derives an optimal sample size selection strategy and gives a numerical example using this same data set. As will become apparent, the argument in this section closely parallels its counterpart in the literature on stratified sampling.

1. ON THE RECONCILIATION OF 'ROWS ONLY' AND 'COLUMNS ONLY' ESTIMATES FOR THE TECHNICAL COEFFICIENTS

In order to discuss the reconciliation of the 'rows only' and 'columns only' estimates for the technical coefficients, this section is organized into two parts. The first of these gives a definition and a brief history of the problem while the second presents the minimum variance technique.[1]

A. An overview of the reconciliation problem

As has been repeatedly indicated, the technical coefficients in a static, open input-output model are typically calculated from the ratio $a_{ij} = Z_{ij}/X_j$, $i,j = 1, \ldots, m$ where Z_{ij} denotes the total value of goods and services transferred from sector i to sector j, X_j represents the total value of output in sector j, and m is the number of sectors in the model. The reconciliation problem arises because there are two ways of observing the Z_{ij}. First, the sales of firms in sector i to firms in sector j may be examined. If the Z_{ij} are measured in this way, then a so-called 'rows only' estimate of a_{ij} is obtained. Alternatively, data concerning the purchases by firms in sector j from firms in sector i may be gathered. This information, when substituted for Z_{ij}, yields 'columns only' estimates for the technical coefficients.[2]

For a given technical coefficient, it would be most improbable if these two estimates were identical. In fact, there are at least two important reasons why they might differ. For example, input-output data are sometimes obtained from a non-exhaustive sampling of the firms within each sector. In this case, there is obviously no reason why the total sales to sector j by the included firms in sector i must equal the total purchases from firms in sector i by the included firms in sector j. Furthermore, even if exhaustive samples are taken, there may be difficulties in removing transport costs from the transactions data.

In some regional input-output studies, both sales and purchases data are collected from each firm so that both 'rows only' and 'columns only' coefficients may be calculated. Clearly, this is more costly than obtaining data on sales or purchases alone. However, it has been argued that the additional information can be used to improve the reliability of the resulting estimates of the technical coefficients.[3]

Nevertheless, the alleged gain from having both 'rows only and columns only' coefficients has, in all probability, never been realized. This is because present methods for combining the two types of estimates have serious weaknesses. Two examples, drawn from the input-output studies of Washington State and West Virginia, provide evidence for this claim. First, consider the study of Washington State which was conducted in 1967 by Bourque and others. They stated that in many of the sectors surveyed, the discrepancy between purchases and sales data on intersectoral flows was significant. Hence, it was necessary to find a way to combine the two sets of information. In order to do this, they reported,

'... each member of the study team met independently with each other member, compared sources, made judgments about reliability, conducted additional field work when necessary, and solved the remaining differences by trading or compromise'.[4]

Bourque's approach to the reconciliation problem leaves much to be desired. It is clearly unsystematic and would be virtually impossible to replicate. In fact, Isard and Langford called the procedure unscientific and likened it to '... a meeting over the kitchen table.'[5] It is worth noting, though, that these last two authors failed to make suggestions which might to used to improve the reconciliation process.

Mierynk's study of West Virginia provides the second illustration of how the reconciliation problem has been handled in a practical setting.[6] As in Bourque's study, he obtained both the 'rows only' and the 'columns only' data on the intersectoral transactions. Then, for both estimates of each technical coefficient, Miernyk constructed what he called reliability quotients. These were based upon considerations such as: (1) the fraction of total sectoral sales accounted for by the sample, (2) the homogeneity of output within the sector, (3) the judgment of interviewers who collected the data, and (4) the 'representativeness' of the sample. Finally, for each technical coefficient, he used these quotients to make a judgment as to which of the two estimates was the more reliable.

Miernyk's approach to the reconciliation problem is just as deficient as Bourque's. For example, the idea of allowing the judgment of interviewers to influence the procedure is somewhat distressing. Furthermore, the meaning of the term reliability was never adequately defined. In particular, does the reliability of an input-output estimate refer to: (1) its mean, (2) its variance, (3) its mean and variance, or (4) something else? The part to follow will attempt to clear up this ambiguity by developing a consistent reconciled estimator with minimum variance properties.

B. A suggestion for improving the reconciliation procedure

In this section, an improved method for handling the reconciliation problem will be developed by calculating the variance for both 'rows only' and 'columns only' estimates of the technical coefficients. It will be shown that knowledge of this measure will aid in avoiding the arbitrary judgments referred to in both of the above studies. In particular, information about the variances of the two estimators can be used to choose the linear combination which minimizes the variance of the reconciled estimator. For expository purposes, this discussion is subdivided as follows: (1) a review of how TSLS can be used to estimate the asymptotic mean and variance of the 'columns only' estimator for the technical coefficients,[7] (2) an extension of these results to obtain the same measures for the 'rows only' estimator, (3) some remarks about an appropriate method for obtaining a reconciled estimator and (4) an illustration of the TSLS reconciliation procedure using the West Virginia data.

1. The 'columns only' estimator

To obtain the 'columns only' estimator of the technical coefficients by TSLS, retain the standard assumptions of input-output analysis outlined in Chapter 2. Further, assume that: (1) all firms in each sector have identical production functions and (2) the inputs and outputs of each firm can be measured only with error. Taken together, these assumptions imply

$$ZT_{ij}^{(r)} = a_{ij}XT_j^{(r)} \tag{4.1}$$

and

$$Z_{ij}^{(r)} = ZT_{ij}^{(r)} + u_{ij}^{(r)} \tag{4.2}$$

$$X_j^{(r)} = XT_j^{(r)} + w_j^{(r)} \tag{4.3}$$

Substituting the relations in (4.2) and (4.3) into (4.1) produces

$$Z_{ij}^{(r)} = a_{ij}X_j^{(r)} + \theta_{ij}^{(r)}; \tag{4.4}$$

$$\theta_{ij}^{(r)} = u_{ij}^{(r)} - a_{ij}w_j^{(r)}$$

where the superscripts refer to the rth firm in sector j, $u_{ij}^{(r)}$ and $w_j^{(r)}$ are each independently and identically distributed (i.i.d.) random variables with mean zero for all r and $ZT_{ij}^{(r)}$ and $XT_j^{(r)}$ are the true values of the measured variables $Z_{ij}^{(r)}$ and $X_j^{(r)}$.

According to the argument in Chapter 3, (4.4) is a member of the system of equations in (3.16). Hence, the parameter a_{ij} may be consistently estimated by TSLS. In particular, this estimate is

$$\hat{a}_{ij}(1) = \frac{X_j^T Q_j (Q_j^T Q_j)^{-1} Q_j^T Z_{ij}}{X_j^T Q_j (Q_j^T Q_j)^{-1} Q_j^T X_j} \tag{4.5}$$

and the asymptotic variance of $\hat{a}_{ij}(1)$ is[8]

$$\sigma_{\hat{a}_{ij}(1)}^2 = \frac{\hat{\sigma}_{\theta_{ij}}^2}{X_j^T Q_j (Q_j^T Q_j)^{-1} Q_j^T X_j} \tag{4.6}$$

where X_j and Z_{ij} are $n_j \times 1$ vectors containing the $X_j^{(r)}$ and $Z_{ij}^{(r)}$ and Q_j is an $n_j \times 2$ matrix of observations on wages and salaries and payments to government. Furthermore, it should be recalled that in order to obtain these estimates, purchases, rather than sales data, are required for the interindustry transactions. Therefore, the relation in (4.5) produces a 'columns only' estimate for the i, j^{th} technical coefficient.

2. The 'rows only' estimator

This technique for estimating the 'columns only' coefficients can be modified to obtain estimates for their 'rows only' counterparts. A description of these modifications will be provided below. First, the discussion will focus on a method of estimating the a_{ij} when the Z_{ij} are measured by observing the sales to sector j by firms in i. The resulting regression equations will be shown to have much the same form as the equations in (3.16). Finally, it will be emphasized that each of these equations is embedded in a larger system and should be estimated by TSLS.

To begin the derivation of an analogue to equation (3.16), sum equation (4.1) over all firms in sector j and divide by $\sum_{r=1}^{N_j} XT_j^{(r)}$. This yields

$$\frac{\sum\limits_{r=1}^{N_j} ZT_{ij}^{(r)}}{\sum\limits_{r=1}^{N_j} XT_j^{(r)}} = a_{ij} \tag{4.7}$$

where N_j denotes that total number of firms in sector j. Next, recall that $ZT_{ij}^{(r)}$ is interpreted as the true purchases of the rth firm in sector j from firms in sector i. This implies that

$$\sum_{r=1}^{N_j} ZT_{ij}^{(r)} = \sum_{r=1}^{N_i} ST_{ij}^{(r)} \tag{4.8}$$

where $ST_{ij}^{(r)}$ represents the true sales by the rth firm in i to firms in sector j. Hence

$$\frac{\sum\limits_{r=1}^{N_i} ST_{ij}^{(r)}}{\sum\limits_{r=1}^{N_j} XT_j^{(r)}} = a_{ij} \tag{4.9}$$

Next, multiplying both sides of (4.9) by the ratio of true total output in sector j to true total output in sector i yields

$$\frac{\sum\limits_{r=1}^{N_i} ST_{ij}^{(r)}}{\sum\limits_{r=1}^{N_i} XT_i^{(r)}} = a_{ij} \frac{\sum\limits_{r=1}^{N_j} XT_j^{(r)}}{\sum\limits_{r=1}^{N_i} XT_i^{(r)}} \tag{4.10}$$

Therefore, if it is assumed that each firm in i sells a constant fraction of its output to firms in sector j, $ST_{ij}^{(r)}$ can be expressed as

$$ST_{ij}^{(r)} = a_{ij} \frac{\sum_{r=1}^{N_j} XT_j^{(r)}}{\sum_{r=1}^{N_i} XT_i^{(r)}} X_i^{(r)} \tag{4.11}$$

As is reasonable, this quantity varies directly with both the i, j^{th} technical coefficient and the level of output in sector j and it varies inversely with the level of output of firms in sector i.

In order to obtain an estimating equation from (4.11), suppose that the intersectoral sales of any firm are subject to measurement error according to

$$S_{ij}^{(r)} = ST_{ij}^{(r)} + v_{ij}^{(r)} \tag{4.12}$$

where $S_{ij}^{(r)}$ represents the observed sales of the rth firm in sector i to firms in sector j and where $v_{ij}^{(r)}$ is a disturbance term which is assumed to be i.i.d. with mean zero for all r. Substituting (4.3) and (4.12) into (4.11) produces

$$S_{ij}^{(r)} = a_{ij} \frac{\sum_{r=1}^{N_j} XT_j^{(r)}}{\sum_{r=1}^{N_i} XT_i^{(r)}} X_i^{(r)} + \epsilon_{ij}^{(r)} \tag{4.13}$$

where

$$\epsilon_{ij}^{(r)} = v_{ij}^{(r)} - a_{ij} \frac{\sum_{r=1}^{N_j} XT_j^{(r)}}{\sum_{r=1}^{N_j} XT_j^{(r)}} w_i^{(r)} \tag{4.14}$$

Finally, since the quantity

$$\sum_{r=1}^{N_j} XT_j^{(r)} \Big/ \sum_{r=1}^{N_i} XT_i^{(r)}$$

is a constant, let

$$b_{ij} = a_{ij} \sum_{r=1}^{N_j} XT_j^{(r)} \Big/ \sum_{r=1}^{N_i} XT_i^{(r)}$$

so that

$$S_{ij}^{(r)} = b_{ij} X_i^{(r)} + \epsilon_{ij}^{(r)};$$
$$\epsilon_{ij}^{(r)} = v_{ij}^{(r)} - b_{ij} w_i^{(r)}$$

(4.15)

Equation (4.15), then, implies that estimates of the a_{ij} can be obtained if: (1) the b_{ij} can be estimated and (2) the ratio $\sum_{r=1}^{N_j} XT_j^{(r)} / \sum_{r=1}^{N_i} XT_i^{(r)}$ is known. As will be demonstrated, the first of these obstacles will not be difficult to overcome. In fact, the b_{ij} can be estimated by TSLS from a system of equations similar to (3.16). However, the second condition, that the ratio $\sum_{r=1}^{N_j} XT_j^{(r)} / \sum_{r=1}^{N_i} XT_i^{(r)}$ be known, will require some further discussion.[9]

In equation (4.15), it should be apparent that OLS will produce biased and inconsistent estimates of the b_{ij} because the $X_i^{(r)}$ are correlated with the error term.[10] Nevertheless, it is possible to obtain consistent estimates for these coefficients. To show how this can be done, consider the following system of equations:

$$X_i^{(r)} = \sum_{j=1}^{m} S_{ij}^{(r)} + SH_i^{(r)} + SG_i^{(r)} + RS_i^{(r)}$$
$$S_{i1}^{(r)} = b_{i1} X_i^{(r)} + \epsilon_{i1}^{(r)}$$
$$S_{i2}^{(r)} = b_{i2} X_i^{(r)} + \epsilon_{i2}^{(r)}$$
$$\vdots \qquad \vdots$$
$$S_{im}^{(r)} = b_{im} X_i^{(r)} + \epsilon_{im}^{(r)}$$

(4.16)

As can be seen, (4.16) is similar in form to the system of equations in (3.16). The first equation in (4.16) is an accounting identity which states that the total output of firm r in sector i must be sold to firms in the m endogenous sectors or to final demand. Here, final demand has been divided into three components: (1) $SH_i^{(r)}$ = sales to households, (2) $SG_i^{(r)}$ = sales to government, and (3) $RS_i^{(r)}$ = all remaining sales to the final demand sector including sales to other firms on capital account and exports. The remaining m relations in (4.16) need no further explanation as they are identical in form to (4.15).

The system of equations in (4.16) will be useful in estimating the b_{ij} if at least one of the above three components of final demand can be measured exactly. Fortunately, this condition should hold for a great many firms. For example, due to various reporting requirements, a firm's sales to government at the state and federal levels may be measured exactly. In addition, sales to households for a particular firm may be accurately computed from its data on retail sales tax collections.[11] Error free measurements on exports and sales to other firms on capital account will probably be much more difficult to obtain. However, this problem is analogous to the one which arose in connection with measuring value added in (3.16) and can be dealt with in much the same way. For instance, if $RS_i^{(r)}$ is suspected of containing measurement error, simply treat this variable as endogenous and add another equation to (4.16) to take this specification into account.

Finally, if one or more components of final demand are known to be error free, the b_{ij} can be estimated by TSLS since each of the estimable relations is identified. This, of course, amounts to using the predicted $\hat{X}_i^{(r)}$ from the reduced form of (4.16) as instruments for the $X_i^{(r)}$. The TSLS estimate of b_{ij} is, then,

$$b_{ij}(1) = \frac{X_i^T P_i (P_i^T P_i)^{-1} P_i^T S_{ij}}{X_i^T P_i (P_i^T P_i)^{-1} P_i^T X_i} \tag{4.17}$$

and the asymptotic variance of $\hat{b}_{ij}$ is estimated by

$$\hat{\sigma}^2_{b_{ij}(1)} = \frac{\hat{\sigma}^2_{\epsilon_{ij}}}{X_i^T P_i (P_i^T P_i)^{-1} P_i^T X_i} \tag{4.18}$$

where X_i and S_{ij} are $n_i x 1$ vectors containing the $X_i^{(r)}$ and $S_{ij}^{(r)}$ and where P_i is an $n_i x 2$ matrix containing the observations on $SH_i^{(r)}$ and $SG_i^{(r)}$; the two variables which are assumed, for the sake of illustration, to be measured exactly.

Now that an estimator for the b_{ij} has been obtained, the corresponding estimates for the a_{ij} must be derived. Recall that from the discussion preceding equation (4.15), a_{ij} can be expressed as

$$a_{ij} = b_{ij} \frac{\displaystyle\sum_{r=1}^{N_i} XT_i^{(r)}}{\displaystyle\sum_{r=1}^{N_i} XT_j^{(r)}} = b_{ij} C_{ij} \tag{4.19}$$

where $C_{ij} = \sum_{r=1}^{N_i} XT_i^{(r)} / \sum_{r=1}^{N_j} XT_j^{(r)}$. As a result, the derivation in question hinges on whether or not C_{ij} is known.

Strictly speaking, the ratio C_{ij} will probably not be known exactly. However, observed analogues for its two components are always calculated in input-output studies. In fact, these analogues, which are usually called control totals, appear in the margin of an input-output table. Obviously, these values cannot be obtained from observing the output of firms which were included in a non-exhaustive sample. Instead, they are usually computed from outside sources. For example, in his study of West Virginia,

Miernyk adjusted state gross receipts tax data in order to obtain the control for each sector.[12]

Under certain conditions, these measured control totals may be used to approximate the C_{ij}. To see why this is true, note that the control totals must be measured by summing the observed total output of each firm in the sector. Further, for the sake of simplicity, assume that these measurements are obtained according to equation (4.3).[13] Denoting the observed counterpart of C_{ij} by $\hat{C}_{ij}$, then

$$\hat{C}_{ij} = \frac{\sum_{r=1}^{N_i} X_i^{(r)}}{\sum_{r=1}^{N_j} X_j^{(r)}} = \frac{\sum_{r=1}^{N_i} (XT_i^{(r)} + w_i^{(r)})}{\sum_{r=1}^{N_j} (XT_j^{(r)} + w_j^{(r)})} \qquad (4.20)$$

Therefore, if N_i and N_j are of even moderate size, $\hat{C}_{ij}$ will be approximately equal to the constant $C_{ij} = \sum_{r=1}^{N_i} XT_i^{(r)} / \sum_{r=1}^{N_j} XT_j^{(r)}$. This is because the sum of the observation errors should be small relative to the true total outputs for both sectors. Based upon this argument, then, a consistent 'rows only' estimator for a_{ij} is

$$\hat{a}_{ij} = \hat{C}_{ij}\hat{b}_{ij}(1) \qquad (4.21)$$

Further, the asymptotic variance of this estimator may be approximated by

$$\hat{\sigma}_{a_{ij}}^2 = \hat{C}_{ij}^2 \hat{\sigma}_{b_{ij}(1)}^2 \qquad (4.22)$$

3. An improved reconciled estimator

At this point, estimation procedures for the 'rows only' and the 'columns only' estimates of the technical coefficients have been discussed. Therefore, it only remains to find an appropriate reconciled estimator. Actually, the task at hand is straightforward if the criterion of minimum variance is used. To demonstrate this proposition, denote the 'rows only' and 'columns only' estimates of the ij^{th} technical coefficient as $\hat{a}_r$ and $\hat{a}_c$, respectively. Further observe that since $\hat{a}_r$ and $\hat{a}_c$ are consistent estimators, a consistent reconciled estimator may be found from

$$\hat{a}_R = q\hat{a}_r + (1 - q)\hat{a}_c \qquad (4.23)$$

where $0 \le q \le 1$ and $\hat{a}_R$ represents the reconciled estimator. Then, by an elementary theorem on the variance of a linear combination of random variables

$$\sigma_{\hat{a}_R}^2 = q^2\, \sigma_{\hat{a}_r}^2 + (1 - q)^2\, \sigma_{\hat{a}_c}^2 + 2q(1 - q)\sigma_{\hat{a}_c \hat{a}_r} \tag{4.24}$$

Hence, to find the value of q which minimizes the variance of $\sigma_{\hat{a}_R}^2$, set the derivative of (4.24) with respect to q equal to zero. This produces

$$q^* = \frac{\sigma_{\hat{a}_c}^2 + \sigma_{\hat{a}_c \hat{a}_r}}{\sigma_{\hat{a}_r}^2 + \sigma_{\hat{a}_c}^2 - 2\sigma_{\hat{a}_c \hat{a}_r}} \tag{4.25}$$

There is at least one feature of equation (4.25) which deserves further comment. This concerns a distinction between choosing q^* for off-diagonal elements in the matrix of technical coefficients and choosing this quantity for diagonal elements. In the case of diagonal elements, it is evident that the estimating equations for $\hat{a}_{ij}(1)$ and $\hat{b}_{ij}(1)$, (4.5) and (4.17), are constructed from observations on the same firms. Hence, it is reasonable to expect $\sigma_{\hat{a}_r \hat{a}_c} \neq 0$. As a result, in practice, this quantity must be calculated from the appropriate regression residuals. On the other hand, for off-diagonal coefficients, the 'rows only' and 'columns only' estimates are obtained from observations on firms in different sectors. Consequently, if measurement errors are uncorrelated between firms in different sectors, then (4.25) reduces to

$$q^* = \frac{\sigma_{\hat{a}_c}^2}{\sigma_{\hat{a}_r}^2 + \sigma_{\hat{a}_c}^2} \tag{4.26}$$

The above procedure for reconciling the 'rows only' and 'columns only' estimates had advantages over the methods used by Bourque and Miernyk. It is clearly more systematic as sample information is substituted for the judgment of the investigator. Moreover, it is based upon conventional statistical principles. But perhaps most importantly, this reconciliation procedure uses the observations on intersectoral transactions to maximum advantage. In particular, any other combination of 'rows only' and 'columns only' estimates will have a higher variance and will, therefore, contain less information about the magnitude of the true technical coefficients.

4. Empirical results

In order to illustrate this improved reconciliation procedure, it was first necessary to obtain TSLS estimates of the technical coefficients for each of the twenty-nine sectors according to the methods described previously in this section. As a practical matter, this amounted to: (1) estimating the a_{ij} and the b_{ij} together with the variances for both sets of coefficients estimates, (2) converting estimates of the b_{ij} to estimates of a_{ij} according to the relation $\hat{a}_{ij} = \hat{C}_{ij}\hat{b}_{ij}$, (3) testing the regression residuals for heteroskedasticity using the Goldfeld-Quandt test, (4) adjusting the data as needed to correct this problem and (5) revising both parameter and coefficient variance estimates in those cases where heteroskedasticity was found to be present. This exercise produced such a large quantity of estimates that no attempt will be made to report them in total. However, a subset of these results are presented in Appendix 4.A (see pages 57–64).

In particular, the 'rows only' estimates, the 'columns only' estimates and the minimum variance reconciled estimates are presented for five rows of the West Virginia input-output table. These rows correspond to the following sectors: (1) Logging and Sawmills, (2) Printing and Publishing, (3) Stone and Clay Products, (4) Wholesale Trade, and (5) All other Retail Trade. These sectors were chosen because the assumptions regarding the exact measurement of the variables: $WS_j^{(r)}$, $PG_j^{(r)}$, $SH_j^{(r)}$, and $SG_j^{(r)}$ appeared to be best satisfied. That is, nearly all observed firms in these five sectors reported wage, salary, and tax payments to the nearest dollar. Also, most of the firms which indicated that they made sales to households provided data on their sales tax collections.

To interpret the tables in Appendix 4.A, it should first be noted that the extreme left hand column gives the row and column index for the technical coefficient under consideration. These indices are taken from Table 3.1. In addition, the second and third columns of these tables provide the 'rows only' and 'columns only' estimates of the technical coefficients indicated in column one according to the TSLS methods summarized by equations (4.5) and (4.17).[14] Standard errors, calculated by taking the square root of the results produced by equations (4.6) and (4.18), are given in parentheses beneath each estimate. Column four, then, presents the minimum variance reconciled estimates together with standard errors for those technical coefficients where both 'rows only' and 'columns only' estimates were computed. These reconciled estimates were constructed using the values of q^* in column five in conjunction with equation (4.26). The values of q^*, in turn, were calculated by assuming that $\sigma_{a_r a_c} = 0$ for off-diagonal technical coefficients and allowing $\sigma_{a_r a_c} \neq 0$ for the diagonal coefficients. Finally, Miernyk's estimates of the technical coefficients are given in the sixth column for comparison purposes.

Before proceeding further, it should be made clear that the purpose of this monograph is neither to condemn nor to vindicate Miernyk's technical coefficient estimates. However, the observation that some of Miernyk's estimates differ substantially from the minimum variance reconciled estimates in all five tables is inescapable. For example, the reconciled estimates for $a_{16,11}$, $a_{32,20}$, and $a_{32,41}$ are more than one hundred times smaller than Miernyk's estimates.

More importantly, though, Appendix 4.A indicates that the reconciliation problem in input-output analysis should not be taken lightly. That is, even a casual examination of these results will reveal a substantial difference between the 'rows only' and 'columns only' estimates of many technical coefficients. In addition, the standard errors for the two types of estimates often differ markedly and do not show a pronounced tendency to be lower for one type of estimate than for another. Therefore, the final table of technical coefficients may be greatly affected by the way in which these discrepancies are reconciled.

These results, to the extent that they are typical, emphasize the need to reconcile 'rows only' and 'columns only' estimates in a systematic way. The proposed minimum variance procedure has two advantages in this regard. First, it ensures that each type of estimate is weighted inversely with the amount of misinformation it is likely to provide. Second, the minimum variance reconciled estimates will always have smaller standard errors than either their 'rows only' or 'columns only' counterparts. This last point is illustrated by comparing the coefficient standard errors in columns two, three, and four in each table.

2. SELECTING SAMPLE SIZES FOR INPUT-OUTPUT ANALYSIS

As was indicated previously, the second problem to be investigated in this chapter concerns the selection of sample sizes for input-output sectors. This topic is important because the data used in regional input-output models are often obtained from a non-exhaustive sampling of firms in the area under study.[15] However, current methods for determining the sample size for each sector are deficient as they are not based upon operational criteria. Therefore, in the section to follow, a systematic method for choosing sample sizes will be offered. Specifically, it will be suggested that a minimum variance criterion be used to guide these decisions. This section is divided into three parts. Part A contains a statement of the sample size problem in input-output analysis and recognizes the progress which others have made toward its solution. Part B, then, outlines the improved method for selecting sample sizes. Finally, Part C contains an illustration of the improved method using the West Virginia data.

A. A survey of the sample size problem

In collecting data to implement an input-output study, a decision must be made as to the number of firms to observe in each sector.[16] Occasionally, the area under study is small enough so that practically all firms can be surveyed.[17] However, the regional input-output literature reveals that it is far more common for the required data to be gathered according to some sort of sampling strategy.

It is interesting to note that a reasonable sampling strategy has been articulated in at least two input-output investigations. First, in his study of West Virginia, Miernyk observed, 'Since the total number of interviews that could be scheduled was subject to a budget constraint, the problem of selecting sample sizes was one of allocating available resources to their most efficient uses.'[18] Second, in reflecting upon their study of the Philadelphia region, Isard and Langford also expressed this idea. They asked, 'How can we identify that point for each sector at which the marginal cost of obtaining additional coverage is equal to the marginal gain?'[19]

Despite the relevance of this proposed sampling strategy, the techniques which have been employed in practical situations to choose the sample size for each sector have been somewhat crude. This state of affairs has arisen primarily because the concept of marginal gain in sampling for input-output models has never been operationalized. Just as in other empirical settings where primary data are gathered, though, the variance might be used to perform this function. That is, Isard and Langford's marginal conditions might be interpreted as: At the margin and for all pairs of sectors, make the ratio of costs per observation equal to the ratio of variance reductions which could be achieved by taking an additional observation.

There are two features of this interpretation which merit some elaboration before proceeding further. First, it does not imply that sample sizes in past input-output studies have been chosen entirely at random. To the contrary, investigators have often taken account of factors such as within sector technological change and extent of product heterogeneity which influence the magnitude of the variance.[20] But without knowing precisely how these factors affect dispersion, this approach is clearly sub-optimal as compared with defining the problem in terms of the variance itself. Second, if past input-output studies are a guide, this suggested interpretation of Isard and Langford's marginal conditions may not appear to be at all promising. As has been indicated throughout the preceding discussion, input-output analysts have failed to calculate standard errors for their estimated technical coefficients. However, from Chapter 3 and the first section of the present chapter, it should be clear that this measure of dispersion may be computed by: (1) assuming that all firms in each sector have identical production and sales functions and (2) estimating the technical coefficients by TSLS.

B. An improved method for selecting sample sizes

Based upon the discussion in Chapter 3, it is now possible to develop an efficient sampling strategy for use in estimating input-output models. Specifically, assuming that TSLS is used as an estimation technique, an asymptotic result will be obtained which shows how the sample size for each sector may be chosen so as to minimize the variance of the estimated technical coefficients.[21] This part: (1) begins with a symbolic statement of the problem, (2) proceeds to a derivation of optimal sample sizes, and (3) concludes with some comments regarding the practical value of this result.

Suppose that a region with m sectors has been designated for an input-output study and let

$$T = \sum_{i=1}^{m} \sum_{j=1}^{m} a_{ij} \qquad \hat{T} = \sum_{i=1}^{m} \sum_{j=1}^{m} \hat{a}_{ij}(1) \tag{4.27}$$

where the a_{ij} are the true technical coefficients and the $\hat{a}_{ij}(1)$ and their corresponding TSLS estimates. Next, in order to simplify the analysis, assume that: (1) the covariance between $\hat{a}_{ij}(1)$ and $\hat{a}_{hl}(1)$ is equal to zero for all $h \neq i$ and $l \neq j$[22] and (2) the $\hat{a}_{ij}(1)$ are 'columns only' estimates.[23] Then, because variances must be non-negative, the least variance set of coefficient estimates may be found by minimizing the sum of variance of the $\hat{a}_{ij}(1)$ subject to a budget constraint. This corresponds to minimizing the loss function

$$L = \plim_{n_j \to N_j} (\hat{T} - T)^2 + \lambda \left(\sum_{j=1}^{m} p_j n_j - B \right) \tag{4.28}$$

In (4.28), n_j denotes the number of observations on sector j, p_j represents the cost of obtaining one observation in sector j, and B is the total budget of the study less costs not associated with sampling.

Optimal sample sizes may be found from the first order conditions for a minimum of (4.28). These conditions are:

$$\sum_{i=1}^{m} \partial \mathrm{Var}(\hat{a}_{i1}(1)) \Big/ \partial n_1 + \lambda p_1 = 0$$

$$\sum_{i=1}^{m} \partial \mathrm{Var}(\hat{a}_{i2}(1)) \Big/ \partial n_2 + \lambda p_2 = 0 \tag{4.29}$$

$$\sum_{i=1}^{m} \partial \mathrm{Var}(\hat{a}_{im}(1)) \Big/ \partial n_m + \lambda p_m = 0$$

$$\sum_{j=1}^{m} p_j n_j - B = 0$$

where $\mathrm{Var}(\hat{a}_{ij}(1))$ denotes the variance of $\hat{a}_{ij}(1)$. They require that, for any

i and j, the ratio of the contribution to variance reduction by the last observation drawn from sector i to its counterpart for sector j be equal to the cost of obtaining observations in sector i normalized by the cost of obtaining observations in sector j. This, in essence, is the mathematical counterpart to the statement by Isard and Langford which was quoted previously.

However, the equations in (4.29) are not yet operational as an expression for the $\sum_{i=1}^{m} \partial \text{Var}(\hat{a}_{ij}(1))/\partial n_j; j = 1, \ldots, m$ is needed. Fortunately, such an expression may be obtained since the asymptotic distribution of $\hat{a}_{ij}(1)$ may be expressed as

$$\sqrt{n_j}(\hat{a}_{ij}(1) - a_{ij}) \sim N\left[0, \sigma^2_{\theta_{ij}} \plim_{n_j \to \infty} \frac{n_j}{X^T Q_j (Q_j^T Q_j)^{-1} Q_j X_j}\right] \qquad (4.30)$$

where, it might be recalled, the notation is carried over from the discussion leading to equation (4.6). Therefore, if

$$\plim_{n_j \to N_j} \frac{n_j}{X^T Q_j (Q_j^T Q_j)^{-1} Q_j^T X_j} \approx \beta_j \qquad (4.31)$$

where β_j is a finite, non-stochastic scalar, the variance of the estimate for the i, j^{th} technical coefficient may be approximated by

$$\text{Var}(\hat{a}_{ij}(1)) = \frac{\sigma^2_{\theta_{ij}} \beta_j}{n_j}$$

$$i,j = 1, \ldots, m \qquad (4.32)$$

and

$$\frac{\partial \text{Var}(\hat{a}_{ij}(1))}{\partial n_j} = -\frac{\sigma^2_{\theta_{ij}} \beta_j}{n_j^2}$$

$$i,j = 1, \ldots, m \qquad (4.33)$$

Finally, substituting the equations in (4.33) into the appropriate member of (4.29) and rearranging terms yields expressions for optimal sample sizes which are of the form

$$n_j^* = \left[\frac{\beta_j \sum_{i=1}^{m} \sigma^2_{\theta_{ij}}}{\lambda p_j}\right]^{1/2} \qquad (4.34)$$

or

$$\frac{n_j^*}{n_i^*} = \left[\frac{p_i \beta_j \sum\limits_{i=1}^{m} \sigma_{\theta_{ij}}^2}{p_j \beta_i \sum\limits_{h=1}^{m} \sigma_{\theta_{hi}}^2} \right]^{1/2} \tag{4.35}$$

As should be evident, the expressions in (4.34) and (4.35) bear a close similarity to their counterparts in stratified sampling.[24] In addition, they contain an identical prescription for selecting sample sizes. That is, n_j^* varies directly with the variances of estimates for the technical coefficients in sector j and varies inversely with the cost of obtaining observations in that sector.

C. Empirical results

The calculation of minimum variance sample sizes according to equations (4.34) and (4.35) may be illustrated using the TSLS estimates of the 'columns only' technical coefficients described in Chapter 3. After adjusting the data where necessary to deal with the heteroskedasticity problem, variances were computed for each coefficient estimate. These variances were then summed in order to obtain the quantities $\hat{\beta}_j \sum_{i=1}^{m} \hat{\sigma}_{\theta_{ij}}^2$, that are required to make the optimal sample size calculations.[25] The $\hat{\beta}_j \sum_{i=1}^{m} \hat{\sigma}_{\theta_{ij}}^2$, which might be called 'sectoral variance estimates,' are given in column three of Table 4.1 for each of the twenty-nine West Virginia input-output sectors from which data were made available.

Under the heading n_j^*/n_{27}^* in column four, Table 4.1 also provides the optimal sample size for each sector relative to the sample size in Sector 27 (All other manufacturing) on the assumption that costs per observation in each sector are identical.[26] Clearly, this assumption is somewhat unrealistic. However, information regarding these costs is presently unavailable. In any case, though, the figures in column four are interpreted as the optimal number of observations in each sector for every observation drawn in Sector 27. These range from a low of 1.705 in Sector 33 (Banking) to a high of 29.189 in Sector 31 (Retail gasoline service stations).

For comparison purposes, Miernyk's actual relative sample sizes are shown in column five of Table 4.1. As can be verified from Table 3.1, these values were obtained by dividing the actual sample size for each sector by its counterpart for Sector 27. From examining columns four and five, it would appear that Miernyk undersampled in every sector relative to the number of observations in 'All other manufacturing.' However, this com-

Table 4.1. Minimum variance relative sample sizes in the West Virginia input-output model.

(1) Sector number	(2) Sector Name	(3) $\beta_j \sum\limits_{i=1}^{m} \hat{\sigma}^2_{\theta_{ij}}$	(4) n_j^*/n_{27}^*	(5) n_j/n_{27}	(6) p_j/p_{27}
2	Underground coal mining	.00104	1.803	.571	9.968
3	Strip and auger mining	.00923	5.371	.714	56.591
6	General contractors (Building)	.05560	13.181	.571	532.891
7	General contractors (Non-building)	.01854	7.612	.357	454.578
8	Special trades contractors	.05282	12.848	.857	224.815
9	Food and kindred products (n.e.c.)	.00192	2.449	.286	73.356
11	Food and kindred products (Bakeries)	.01233	6.207	.429	209.389
14	Logging and sawmills	.03110	9.858	1.286	58.798
15	Furniture and other wood fabrication	.02183	8.259	.929	79.066
16	Printing and publishing	.00791	4.972	1.357	13.422
19	Glass	.00133	2.039	.643	10.054
20	Stone and clay products	.01226	6.190	1.214	26.014
21	Primary metal products	.01275	6.312	.714	76.614
22	Fabricated metal products	.00499	3.949	.857	21.239
23	Machinery (except electrical)	.00245	2.767	.714	15.022
24	Electrical machinery and apparatus	.00124	1.969	.357	30.520
27	All other manufacturing	.00032	1.000	1.000	1.000
29	Wholesale trade	.00596	4.316	2.214	3.800
31	Retail gasoline service stations	.27263	29.189	.643	2060.912
32	All other retail	.01523	6.899	2.643	6.806
33	Banking	.00093	1.705	.643	6.246
36	Real estate	.00353	3.321	.643	26.685
38	Hotels and other lodging places	.02235	8.357	.357	547.994
39	Medical and legal services	.00972	5.511	1.357	16.494
41	All other services	.05359	12.941	1.000	167.469
43	Trucking and warehousing	.03946	11.105	.286	1507.619
44	All other transportation	.01070	5.783	.571	102.553
45	Communications	.00174	2.332	.500	21.750
47	Gas companies and systems	.14028	20.937	.500	1753.500

parison must be tempered for three reasons. First, and most obviously, Miernyk drew his sample before looking at the data. Second, as was indicated previously, the sales data which he collected were not used in the illustration at hand. If these data had been used, the optimal sample sizes in column four would almost certainly change. Third, costs per observation in each of the West Virginia sectors may have differed.

This last problem of differing costs per observation in the various sectors is at least partially remedied by the calculations shown in column six of Table 4.1. These figures were obtained by assuming that Miernyk had selected minimum variance sample sizes and then calculating the implied relative costs per observation. This was accomplished by rewriting equation (4.35) as

$$
\frac{p_j}{p_i} = \left[\frac{\beta_j \sum_{i=1}^{m} \sigma_{\theta_{ij}}^2}{\beta_i \sum_{k=1}^{m} \sigma_{\theta_{ki}}^2} \right] \left[\frac{n_i}{n_j} \right]^2
\tag{4.36}
$$

where once again, $i = 27$ and where the values of n_{27}/n_j were obtained from Miernyk's actual relative sample sizes shown in column five of Table 4.1. These figures show that if Miernyk's sample sizes were optimal, then, relative to Sector 27, observations must have been at least six times as expensive to collect in the other twenty-eight sectors. Furthermore, observations must have been more than 2060 times as costly in the 'Retail gasoline service station' sector as in 'All other manufacturing.'

As with other optimal sampling rules, and in all fairness to Miernyk, the one at hand suffers from an apparent weakness. That is, in addition to the sampling costs, n_j^* is seen to depend upon the true and, consequently, unknown variances of the $\hat{a}_{ij}(1)$. To be sure, these parameters are estimable, but only after a sample has been drawn.

However, there are at least two reasons why this problem may not be as serious as it appears. First of all, from (4.35), the ratio, n_j^*/n_i^*, may be approximated if only the relative magnitudes for the variances of the $\hat{a}_{ij}(1)$ are known. Second, there are important sources of information about these variances which could be tapped. In particular, an analysis of the data collected in past input-output studies may provide a clue as to which are 'high variance' and which are 'low variance' sectors. Naturally, the usefulness of this suggestion may be limited by the great diversity of sector definitions which have been employed in the past. However, it may be of great benefit to consider these variances in cases where an input-output study is replicated using a similar industrial classification.

NOTES

1. A review of the standard assumptions of input-output analysis is omitted in this chapter. If a discussion of these assumptions is desired, see Section I of Chapter 2.
2. Some regional input-output studies make use of only one type of estimate. For an example of a study using only 'rows only' estimates, see W. Lee Hansen and Charles M. Tiebout, 'An Intersectoral Flows Analysis of the California Economy,' *Review of Economics and Statistics*, XLV, November, 1963, 409–418. For an example of the exclusive use of 'columns only' coefficients, see Walter Isard and Thomas Langford, *Regional Input-Output Study: Recollections, Reflections, and Diverse Notes on the Philadelphia Experience*, Cambridge, Mass., MIT Press, 1971.

3. William H. Miernyk, *et al.*, *Simulating Regional Economic Development*, Lexington, Mass., D. C. Heath, 1970, p. 18.
4. Phillip J. Bourque, *et al.*, *The Washington Economy: An Input-Output Study*, Seattle, Washington, University of Washington, 1967, p. 6.
5. Isard and Langford, *Regional Input-Output Study*, p. 62.
6. Miernyk, *Simulating Regional Economic Development*, p. 18.
7. For a more complete discussion of 'columns only' estimation of the technical coefficients by TSLS, see Section 3 of Chapter 3.
8. Phoebus J. Dhrymes, *Econometrics: Statistical Foundations and Applications*, New York, Harper and Row, 1970, p. 187.
9. This is momentarily postponed to the end of this part, so that the estimation procedure for the b_{ij} may be fully explained.
10. J. Johnston, *Econometric Methods*, New York, McGraw-Hill, 1972, pp. 281–91.
11. These arguments concerning the quality of measurement on the three components of final demand are not intended as general statements about all input-output sectors. For example, some firms making sales to households may sell goods and services which are exempt from retail sales taxation. In addition, collection on government sales contracts may lag behind the actual transfer of goods. These, and other, measurement problems must be handled on a sector by sector basis. Finally, if for certain sectors, it is reasonable to assume that the total output of each firm can be measured exactly, then unbiased estimates of the b_{ij} can be estimated from an OLS regression of $S_{ij}^{(r)}$ on $X_i^{(r)}$.
12. Miernyk, *Simulating Regional Economic Development*, p. 17.
13. Obviously, these measurements may not be obtained according to (4.3) because they are assumed to be computed from outside sources. However, making this distinction explicit would only complicate the notation without affecting the result.
14. It should be noted that 'columns only' estimates for all technical coefficients in the three tables were not possible due to lack of data. To determine which coefficients were affected, compare the column indices in Appendix 4.A against the sectors listed in Table 3.1 for which no questionnaires were provided.
15. Harry W. Richardson, *Input-Output and Regional Economics*, New York, John Wiley and Sons, 1972, p. 96–100.
16. It might be noted that in some regional input-output studies, the a_{ij} are calculated from secondary sources; such as by adjusting national technical coefficients. For discussions of how this can be done, see Stanislaw Czamanski and Emil E. Malizia, 'Applicability and Limitations in the Use of National Input-Output Tables for Regional Studies,' *The Regional Science Association Papers* XXIII, 1969; William A. Schaffer and Kong Chu, 'Nonsurvey Techniques for Constructing Regional Interindustry Models,' *The Regional Science Association Papers*, XXIII, 1969; And Albert J. Walderhaug, 'State Input-Output Tables Derived from National Data,' *American Statistical Association*, Proceedings, 1971. However, the section at hand is mainly concerned with input-output studies based upon primary data.
17. For example, see Werner Hochwald, Herbert E. Striner, and Sidney Sonenblum, *Local Impact of Foreign Trade*, Washington, D.C., National Planning Association, 1960.
18. William H. Miernyk, 'Sampling Techniques in Making Regional Industry Forecasts,' *Applications of Input-Output Analysis*, ed. A. P. Carter and A. Brody, Amsterdam, North-Holland, 1970.
19. Walter Isard and Thomas Langford, *Regional Input-Output Study: Recollections, Reflections, and Diverse Notes on the Philadelphia Experience*, Cambridge, Mass., MIT Press, 1971, p. 55.
20. For example, see Tong Hun Lee, John R. Moore, and David P. Lewis, *A Report on the Tennessee Interindustry Study*, Knoxville, Tenn., University of Tennessee Press, 1973, p. 29; and William H. Miernyk, *et al.*, *Simulating Regional Economic Development*, Lexington, Mass., D. C. Heath, 1970, p. 3–17.
21. To avoid needless repetition, all subsequent discussion of the sampling distribution of $\hat{a}_{ij}(1)$ refers to its asymptotic sampling distribution.
22. This proposition is not defended too vigorously. However, it seems to be necessary in order to produce manageable results.

23. As will become apparent, the results to follow are easily generalizable to either the 'rows only' estimates of a_{ij} or to a reconciled estimate of this parameter.

24. Morris H. Hansen; William N. Hurwitz and William G. Madow, *Sample Survey Methods and Theory*, Vol. I, New York, John Wiley and Sons, 1953, p. 206–13.

25. Note that the quantities $\hat{\beta}_j \sum_{i=1}^{m} \hat{\sigma}_{\theta_{ij}}^2$ are just the observed TSLS estimated analogues of the $\beta_j \sum_{i=1}^{m} \sigma_{\theta_{ij}}^2$.

26. It might also be noted that Sector 27 was chosen to be 'numeraire' for two reasons. First, the sectoral variance for this sector $\hat{\beta}_{27} \sum_{i=1}^{m} \hat{\sigma}_{\theta_{ij27}}^2$ was the smallest of the twenty-nine. Second, a numeraire had to be chosen since the sampling budget in the West Virginia study was not known, and as a consequence, the Lagrange multiplier, λ, in equation (4.34) could not be eliminated. Hence, absolute sample sizes could not be calculated.

Appendix 4.A

Estimates of the technical coefficients for the row corresponding to the logging and sawmills sector

Row, column index	'Rows only' estimate	'Columns only' estimate	Reconciled estimate	q^*	Miernyk's estimate
14,1	.37284-02 (.13481-01)				.00909
14,2	.27064-01 (.10400-01)	.39158-02 (.23174-02)	.50108-02 (.22619-02)	.04730	.00649
14,3		.10788-02 (.13278-02)			.00064
14,4	.46111-03 (.22355-03)				.00008
14,5					.00805
14,6	.39000-03 (.14106-02)				.00302
14,7					.00124
14,8		.17280-01 (.11460-01)			.00987
14,14	.45963-01 (.21788-01)	.13306-00 (.43201-01)	.59225-01 (.18442-01)	.74835	.15534
14,15	.15497-00 (.12319-00)	.91322-01 (.23170-01)	.93497-01 (.22771-01)	.03417	.13416
14,18	.40687-04 (.11919-02)				.00079
14,23		.27729-05 (.14642-03)			.00027
14,29	.13327-03 (.52066-04)	.59261-05 (.95089-04)	.10390-03 (.45668-04)	.76934	
14,32		.13226-04 (.14650-03)			
14,39					.00002
14,40					.00026
14,43					.00094

Estimates of the technical coefficients for the row corresponding
to the printing and publishing sector

Row, column index	'Rows only' estimate	'Columns only' estimate	Reconciled estimate	q^*	Miernyk's estimate
16,1	.20564-04				
	(.85170-03)				.00013
16,2	.33965-04	.60432-03	.21862-03		
	(.29910-03)	(.43228-03)	(.24596-03)	.67625	.00078
16,3		.10620-04			
		(.10874-04)			.00002
16,4					.00256
16,5					.00044
16,6	.24366-03	.26306-02	.11939-02		
	(.61416-03)	(.75518-03)	(.47648-03)	.60190	.00257
16,7	.14796-03	.44503-03	.43853-03		
	(.55779-03)	(.83414-04)	(.82497-04)	.02187	.00101
16,8	.10526-04	.21344-02	.13651-03		
	(.43471-03)	(.17311-02)	(.42162-03)	.94068	.00051
16,9	.35775-03	.74164-01	.48096-02		
	(.10471-02)	(.41329-02)	(.10150-02)	.93968	.00262
16,10	.35789-05				
	(.18907-04)				.00091
16,11	.58619-05	.25071-03	.63512-05		
	(.31276-04)	(.69894-03)	(.31245-04)	.99800	.00147
16,12	.10980-03				
	(.34183-03)				.00812
16,13	.38101-03				
	(.15872-02)				.00395
16,14	.45996-04	.56006-04	.55989-04		
	(.18872-02)	(.77628-04)	(.77562-04)	.00169	.00032
16,15		.10497-02			
		(.27639-03)			.00209
16,16	.70790-04	.40595-01	.56577-02		
	(.74099-02)	(.16860-01)	(.69832-02)	.86213	.26199
16,17	.57252-04				
	(.16860-01)				.00121
16,18					.00124
16,19	.12024-02	.29713-03			
	(.40870-03)	(.18629-02)			.00045
16,20	.20191-03	.69388-03	.24338-03		
	(.64192-03)	(.21158-02)	(.61427-03)	.91571	.00258
16,21		.54051-03			
		(.31252-03)			.00013
16,22	.24822-04	.47939-02	.80495-03		
	(.10251-02)	(.23180-02)	(.93752-03)	.83642	.00270
16,23	.13717-03				
	(.17563-02)				.00087
16,24	.25172-04	.55853-04	.54207-04		
	(.10395-02)	(.24747-03)	(.24074-03)	.05364	.00104
16,25	.12421-03				
	(.44694-03)				.00028
16,26					.00046
16,27	.72309-03	.18130-02	.11732-02		
	(.20137-02)	(.23975-02)	(.15420-02)	.58635	.00250
16,28	.15699-03				
	(.52769-03)				.00060

Row, column index	'Rows only' estimate	'Columns only' estimate	Reconciled estimate	q^*	Miernyk's estimate
16,29	.20864-03 (.46897-03)	.67695-03 (.35120-03)	.50868-03 (.28111-03)	.35931	.00083
16,30	.18685-02 (.40808-02)				.04138
16,31	.73247-04 (.30700-03)	.37938-03 (.33307-03)	.21387-03 (.22574-03)	.54066	.00239
16,32	.19730-02 (.50075-02)	.24075-01 (.12112-02)	.22853-01 (.11773-02)	.65527	.02312
16,33	.44177-03 (.11271-02)	.17330-01 (.44475-02)	.14609-02 (.10926-02)	.93965	.00547
16,34	.65243-05 (.24049-03)				.01102
16,35	.37754-04 (.13258-03)				.00023
16,36	.25645-03 (.10200-02)	.18575-01 (.72254-02)	.61438-03 (.10100-02)	.98046	.02568
16,37					.00397
16,38	.29675-03 (.11371-02)	.27385-03 (.40827-03)	.27647-03 (.38425-03)	.11419	.00147
16,39	.19033-03 (.45639-03)	.34771-02 (.21848-02)	.32776-03 (.44675-03)	.95819	.00065
16,40	.15051-04 (.10835-02)				.00473
16,41	.13204-03 (.45676-03)	.42843-02 (.11490-02)	.70385-03 (.42445-03)	.86354	.00489
16,42	.20410-04 (.72593-04)				.00007
16,43	.11648-03 (.41448-03)	.90314-02 (.19789-02)	.49113-03 (.40568-03)	.95797	.00472
16,44		.36220-03 (.26883-03)			.00026
16,45	.87944-03 (.24547-02)				.00197
16,46	.42670-04 (.17162-02)				.00285
16,47	.44989-05 (.17541-03)	.70067-03 (.54526-05)	.70000-03 (.54500-05)	.00097	.00051
16,48	.17208-03 (.17224-01)				.00178

Estimates of the technical coefficients for the row corresponding to the stone and clay products sector

Row, column index	'Rows only' estimate	'Columns only' estimate	Reconciled estimate	q^*	Miernyk's estimate
20,1	.13216-02				
	(.74925-02)				.00742
20,2	.75033-05	.99945-03	.99619-03		
	(.10295-01)	(.59150-03)	(.59053-03)	.00329	.00380
20,5					.00011
20,6	.61348-02	.37003-02	.37515-02		
	(.28523-01)	(.414787-02)	(.41346-02)	.02101	.09769
20,7	.211172-01	.62761-02	.95403-02		
	(.24151-01)	(.12984-01)	(.11474-01)	.21913	.05763
20,8	.11112-03	.86966-04	.92580-04		
	(.26780-02)	(.14736-02)	(.12910-02)	.23242	.00116
20,9	.70984-03				
	(.56879-03)				.00004
20,13	.55618-04				
	(.13021-03)				
20,14	.21151-03				
	(.12708-03)				.00002
20,15	.97251-04				
	(.20399-03)				
20,16	.17310-03				
	(.10705-03)				
20,17	.53585-04				
	(.88788-03)				.00116
20,20	.59751-03	.47363-02	.34832-02		
	(.14397-01)	(.90809-02)	(.74839-02)	.30273	.01849
20,21	.12973-02				
	(.58751-03)				.00001
20,27					.00001
20,29	.17020-04	.97991-05	.97991-05		
	(.62693-02)	(.79939-05)	(.79939-05)	.00000	
20,36	.82685-03	.46882-01	.10232-02		
	(.52138-03)	(.79687-02)	(.52027-03)	.99574	.00005
20,40	.40324-03				
	(.72768-03)				.00072
20,41	.10636-02				
	(.26369-02)				.00236
20,43	.37579-02				
	(.80919-03)				.00021
20,45					.00175
20,46	.12154-03				
	(.22205-04)				.00260
20,47	.20378-03				
	(.30179-02)				.00130
20,48	.28224-02				
	(.12458-01)				.00555

Estimates of the technical coefficients for the row corresponding
to the wholesale trade sector

Row, column index	'Rows only' estimate	'Columns only' estimate	Reconciled estimate	q^*	Miernyk's estimate
29,1					.04576
29,2	.18686-01	.49873-01	.45328-01		
	(.24899-01)	(.10284-01)	(.95052-02)	.14573	.01265
29,3	.24586-03	.97548-01	.98844-03		
	(.10875-02)	(.12401-01)	(.10833-02)	.99237	.01921
29,4	.76024-02				
	(.28631-01)				.01074
29,5	.13307-00				
	(.30355-00)				
					.02251
29,6	.37709-01	.21840-00	.55003-01		
	(.20622-01)	(.63388-01)	(.19610-01)	.90429	.01693
29,7	.13322-01	.23135-01	.16391-01		
	(.16481-01)	(.24433-01)	(.13663-01)	.68728	.01599
29,8	.75972-02	.11429-00	.21181-01		
	(.19234-01)	(.50356-01)	(.17968-01)	.87268	.02951
29,9		.36115-02			
		(.21504-01)			.03204
29,10					.00605
29,11		.10303-01			
		(.11117-02)			.02408
29,12					.01260
29,13					.00199
29,14	.14024-01	.47973-02	.48989-02		
	(.50182-01)	(.52939-02)	(.52647-02)	.01101	.01956
29,15		.27672-01			
		(.18781-01)			.00779
29,16		.51278-02			
		(.19423-02)			.00226
29,17	.19528-01				
	(.14013-01)				.00795
29,18					.00459
29,19		.30408-02			
		(.35320-02)			.01048
29,20	.13459-02	.64692-01	.27471-02		
	(.45602-02)	(.30320-01)	(.45095-02)	.97788	.01078
29,21	.68866-05	.11133-03	.73684-04		
	(.35177-03)	(.26408-03)	(.21119-03)	.36044	.00485
29,22		.47755-02			
		(.19998-02)			.01158
29,23		.56214-01			
		(.16175-01)			.00895
29,24		.11010-01			
		(.11741-02)			.00495
29,25					.00225
29,26					.00917
29,27		.60039-03			
		(.12712-02)			.00155

Row, column index	'Rows only' estimate	'Columns only' estimate	Reconciled estimate	q^*	Miernyk's estimate
29,28	.11437-03 (.22483-01)				.05279
29,29	.59884-07 (.90057-03)	.58465-03 (.88319-03)	.31181-03 (.84972-03)	.46666	.01633
29,30	.88727-04 (.30176-00)				.00533
29,31	.43114-00 (.23984-01)	.20625-00 (.10545-00)	.20668-00 (.10535-01)	.00193	.01104
29,32	.31487-01 (.31488-01)	.41439-01 (.17037-01)	.35318-01 (.10570-01)	.61507	.00205
29,33		.38990-02 (.46655-02)			.00046
29,34					.00052
29,35					.00035
29,36		.75431-04 (.353660-03)			.00821
29,37					.00008
29,38	.68343-05 (.16400-01)	.79949-01 (.84021-01)	.294008-02 (.16096-01)	.96330	.01487
29,39	.31456-06 (.44466-03)	.90054-02 (.35010-02)	.14327-03 (.44112-03)	.98412	.00944
29,40	.97329-03 (.31886-02)				.01622
29,41	.74897-04 (.15910-03)	.26586-02 (.46356-02)	.77937-04 (.15901-03)	.99882	.01724
29,42					.00256
29,43	.92845-01 (.10815-00)	.34004-00 (.11306-00)	.21096-00 (.78152-01)	.52219	.05333
29,44		.13012-01 (.74014-02)			.00271
29,45		.23653-07 (.12778-04)			.00035
29,46	.56486-01 (.34212-01)				.00477
29,47	.48892-07 (.10298-03)	.38394-02 (.28783-04)	.35612-02 (.27721-04)	.07246	.00119
29,48					.01265

Estimates of the technical coefficients for the row corresponding to the all other retail trade sector

Row, column index	'Rows only' estimate	'Columns only' estimate	Reconciled estimate	q^*	Miernyk's estimate
32,1	.11568-03 (.22269-02)				.00445
32,2	.20462-04 (.35179-03)				.00286
32,3		.16805-04 (.98387-04)			.00155
32,4					.00842
32,5	.42206-04 (.41023-03)				.00559
32,6	.27134-02 (.76250-02)	.17581-02 (.14458-02)	.17913-02 (.14205-02)	.03471	.00044
32,7	.42040-04 (.88885-03)	.24967-03 (.77765-03)	.15965-03 (.45723-04)	.43357	.00184
32,8	.20688-04 (.43420-03)	.78073-02 (.76453-02)	.45723-04 (.43350-03)	.99678	.00049
32,9		.36202-05 (.43528-04)			.00405
32,10	.18929-06 (.52654-05)				.00339
32,11		.20770-02 (.20535-02)			.00976
32,12					.00139
32,14		.72055-03 (.79619-03)			.00107
32,15		.33989-03 (.23601-01)			.00062
32,16	.24096-04 (.67041-03)	.54423-02 (.23333-02)	.43728-03 (.64434-03)	.92374	.00422
32,17	.23264-04 (.22587-03)				.00307
32,18					.00053
32,19					.00275
32,20	.22386-05 (.62260-04)	.88932-03 (.13733-02)	.40581-05 (.62196-04)	.99795	.00475
32,21		.11262-03 (.10534-03)			.00253
32,22		.10067-02 (.43371-03)			.00388
32,23	.65640-05 (.18257-03)	.36500-03 (.23230-03)	.14343-03 (.14354-03)	.61817	.00100
32,24		.10994-02 (.72552-03)			.00341
32,25					.00105
32,27	.18133-04 (.10316-03)	.12121-03 (.33452-03)	.27084-04 (.98579-04)	.91316	.00019
32,28	.54230-03 (.17038-02)				.00150
32,29		.20585-03 (.14897-03)			.00323

Row, column index	'Rows only' estimate	'Columns only' estimate	Reconciled estimate	q^*	Miernyk's estimate
32,30	.37230-05 (.10355-03)				.00059
32,31	.11435-05 (.31844-04)	.95533-03 (.72177-03)	.29972-05 (.31813-04)	.99806	.00106
32,32	.38039-03 (.10136-02)	.20158-02 (.51091-03)	.16992-02 (.47030-03)	.19358	.00291
32,33	.15044-03 (.14604-02)	.27677-02 (.17841-02)	.12005-02 (.11302-02)	.59879	.00286
32,34	.54960-04 (.52379-03)				.00118
32,35	.43788-04 (.42491-03)				.00040
32,36	.20145-03 (.19276-02)	.76641-03 (.33920-03)	.14944-03 (.33407-03)	.03004	.00660
32,37					.00050
32,38	.89713-04 (.56308-03)	.52272-02 (.75869-02)	.11786-03 (.56154-03)	.99452	.00684
32,39	.84937-04 (.82411-03)	.28553-03 (.10220-02)	.16398-03 (.64152-03)	.60598	.00630
32,40	.34003-03 (.21873-02)				.00737
32,41	.67412-05 (.65428-04)	.43989-01 (.24726-01)	.70492-05 (.654281-04)	.9999	.01079
32,42					.00051
32,43		.42472-02 (.16689-02)			.00138
32,44		.69040-02 (.46448-02)			.00043
32,45	.75786-04 (.73425-03)	.58152-02 (.51753-02)	18903-03 (.72697-03)	.98027	.00162
32,46	.19319-04 (.18488-03)				.00060
32,47	.15959-04 (.15378-03)	.19821-02 (.15056-04)	.19634-02 (.14984-04)	.00949	.00046
32,48	.38948-04 (.39942-03)				.05772

5. The conditions for eliminating first order aggregation bias in input-output models when technical coefficients are estimated by a member of the k-class

Over the past twenty-five years, the problem of aggregation bias in input-output analysis has been investigated by many scholars.[1] This interest has arisen largely because aggregation bias has important consequences for input-output forecasting: In particular, it may cause the estimates of total output to be inaccurate. However, judging from the current literature on this subject, there is little that can be done to remove these inaccuracies. As has been pointed out repeatedly, the conditions which have been established for zero aggregation bias are quite restrictive and unlikely to be satisfied in practical situations.

The present chapter, though, examines the aggregation problem from an entirely new viewpoint. Essentially, it will be argued that the magnitude of this problem is influenced by the statistical technique used to estimate the technical coefficients. That is, it will be shown that alternative estimators of these parameters are associated with different values of aggregation bias. But more importantly, this fact will be used to demonstrate that Theil's first order aggregation bias may vanish if the appropriate estimator is used to obtain values for the technical coefficients.[2]

At first, this line of argument may appear to be somewhat out of place as the proponents of input-output analysis have seldom considered alternatives to the ratio method for calculating the technical coefficients. However, as was indicated in Chapter 3, members of the k-class, such as two-stage least squares may be used to estimate these parameters. Hence, a wide range of statistical techniques is available to perform this function.

In the discussion to follow, the aggregation properties of the ratio estimator and the k-class estimators will be studied. Specifically, the objective of this effort is to determine the conditions under which first order aggregation bias may be eliminated using both types of estimation techniques. To pursue this goal, this chapter is organized into two sections. In Section 1, some background will be provided by reviewing the aggregation problem in an input-output context. Section 2, then, presents two classes of results. First of all, to put the remaining discussion in perspective, the conditions under which the ratio estimator will eliminate first order aggregation bias will be derived. These conditions were established in earlier papers by Theil and Morimoto.[3] Second, two new theorems on eliminating first order aggregation bias using k-class estimators will be proved. These theorems indicate that the opportunities for eliminating this source of error are much wider than is generally realized.

1. INPUT-OUTPUT ANALYSIS AND THE AGGREGATION PROBLEM

As was indicated previously, the purpose of this section is to provide a foundation for the remainder of the chapter. This will be done by: (1) reviewing the assumptions of the static, open input-output model and demonstrating how aggregation causes them to be violated, and (2) describing the way in which aggregation causes inaccuracies in an input-output forecast, and defining the concept of aggregation bias in terms of these inaccuracies.

A. The assumptions of input-output analysis and the effect of aggregation

As was indicated in Chapter 2, input-output analysts typically make three assumptions about the production processes in an economy under study: (1) each sector produces a homogeneous product; (2) there are neither external economies nor diseconomies in production, and (3) the level of output in each sector uniquely determines the quantity of each input which is purchased. However, in treating the aggregation problem, it is necessary to distinguish between micro sectors which are assumed to obey these assumptions and the so-called macro sectors which do not. As will become clear momentarily, the macro sectors are simply combinations of micro sectors. Unfortunately, this distinction requires some additions to the notation established in the preceding chapters. In particular,

χ_h = total value of output in the hth micro sector

ζ_{lh} = total value of output transferred from sector l to sector h

ψ_h = value added in sector h.

Using the assumptions in the previous paragraph, these variables are related by

$$\zeta_{lh} = \alpha_{lh}\chi_h + v_{lh} \qquad l,h = 1, \ldots, N \tag{5.1}$$

where α_{lh} are micro technical coefficients which are interpreted as the minimum value of output from micro sector l required to produce one dollar's worth of output in sector h and where v_{lh} is a random disturbance term which has been included to capture the effects of either: (1) errors in measuring any of the $N(N + 1)$ variables or (2) factors affecting χ_h or ζ_{lh} but which have been omitted from (5.1).[4] Finally, if all firms in each micro sector are assumed to have identical Leontief type production functions, then α_{lh} may be estimated from the stochastic equation

$$\zeta_{lh}^{(p)} = \alpha_{lh} \chi_h^{(p)} + v_{lh}^{(p)} \qquad l, h = 1, \ldots, N \tag{5.2}$$

where the superscript denotes the pth firm in the hth micro sector.[5]

For most any economic area, the total number of micro sectors is likely to be very large. Consequently, in empirical input-output models, analysts are generally forced to aggregate or combine some micro sectors owing both to data availability and to cost considerations. In other words, they construct a macro analogue to (5.1) which might be written as

$$Z_{ij} = a_{ij}X_j + u_{ij} \qquad i, j = 1, \ldots, M \tag{5.3}$$

where $M < N$ and where all variables are just the macro counterparts to the arguments in (5.1). The remainder of this chapter will consider the consequences of aggregation. In this discussion, it will be assumed that the a_{ij} are estimated according to

$$Z_{ij}^{(r)} = a_{ij} X_j^{(r)} + u_{ij}^{(r)} \qquad i, j = 1, \ldots, M \tag{5.4}$$

where, once again, the superscript denotes the rth firm in macro sector j.

B. The aggregation bias in an input-output forecast

With this background established, it is now possible to be more specific about the problems which aggregation may cause in input-output forecasting. This will be accomplished by: (1) specifying both a macro and a micro input-output model and deriving total output forecasts for each, (2) comparing these forecasts in order to show that, in general, they will not be equal, (3) defining aggregation bias in terms of these discrepancies and (4) illustrating the relation between aggregation bias and other sources of error that give rise to these discrepancies.

Based upon equations (5.1) and (5.2) the micro model may be written in matrix notation as[6]

$$X_N = A_{NN}X_N + Y_N + U_N \tag{5.5}$$

and from equations (5.3) and (5.4), the macro model is specified as

$$X_M = A_{MM}X_M + Y_M + U_M \tag{5.6}$$

where[7]

$$
\begin{aligned}
A_{NN} &= \{\alpha_{lh}\} & A_{MM} &= \{a_{ij}\} \\
X_N &= \{\chi_l\} & X_M &= \{X_i\} \\
U_N &= \{v_l\} & U_M &= \{u_i\}
\end{aligned}
\tag{5.7}
$$

and where Y_N and Y_M are vectors containing the level of final demand for the N micro sectors and M macro sectors, respectively; while, from equations (5.2) and (5.4) $\sum_p\sum_h v_{lh}^{(p)} = v_l$ and $\sum_r\sum_j u_{ij}^{(r)} = u_i$.

Next, assume that forecasts for total output are desired for a future year. To this effect, suppose that final demands in that year are known for both the micro and macro models and denote them by T_N and T_M, where

$$T_N = \{\tau_h\} \qquad T_M = \{t_i\} \tag{5.8}$$

Then, two forecasts may be obtained: The first is

$$X_N = (I_{NN} - A_{NN})^{-1}\, T_N \tag{5.9}$$

which results from applying T_N to the systematic part of the reduced form or Leontief inverse of (5.5), and the second, which is

$$X_M = (I_{MM} - A_{MM})^{-1} T_M \tag{5.10}$$

derives from an analogous operation on equation (5.6).

However, since the equations of (5.5) and (5.6) have been assumed to be stochastic, there will be uncertainty associated with measuring the elements of both A_{NN} and A_{MM}. As a result, neither the predictions in (5.9) nor (5.10) are possible unless U_M and U_N are null vectors. In fact, both X_N and X_M will differ from the actual prediction which would arise in an empirical setting. This prediction might be written as

$$\hat{X}_M = (I_{MM} - \hat{A}_{MM})^{-1} T_M \tag{5.11}$$

where $\hat{A}_{MM}$ is an estimator of A_{MM}. It is termed the 'actual prediction' because, as was pointed out earlier, input-output analysts are typically forced to estimate the parameters of the macro model under conditions of incomplete information.

It is interesting to compare the prediction of X_N in (5.9) with the prediction of $\hat{X}_M$ in (5.11) because this comparison: (1) will be useful in defining the concepts of total aggregation bias and first order aggregation bias and (2) will illustrate the relation between these concepts and other types of error such as estimation error inherent in input-output forecasting.[7] Moreover, the comparison is not difficult if the following aggregation matrix is introduced. Let

$$
J_{MN} = \begin{bmatrix}
1 \ldots. 10 \ldots. 0 \ldots. 0 \ldots. 0 \\
0 \ldots. 01 \ldots. 1 \ldots. 0 \ldots. 0 \\
\cdots\cdots\cdots\cdots\cdots\cdots\cdots\cdots \\
0 \ldots. 00 \ldots. 0 \ldots. 1 \ldots. 1
\end{bmatrix}
\tag{5.12}
$$

where the ith row of J_{MN} contains a unit for each micro sector that is to be included in the ith macro sector and a zero for each micro sector that is to be excluded. Under this specification, then

$$
\begin{aligned}
X_M &= J_{MN} X_N \\
T_M &= J_{MN} T_N
\end{aligned}
\tag{5.13}
$$

Now, the predictions generated by equations (5.9) and (5.11) may be more explicitly compared. First, note that the micro predictions in (5.9) may be aggregated to form

$$
X_M = J_{MN} X_N = J_{MN} (I_{NN} - A_{NN})^{-1} T_N
\tag{5.14}
$$

Subtracting (5.14) from (5.11), then, produces

$$
\hat{X}_M - X_M = (I_{MM} - \hat{A}_{MM})^{-1} T_M - J_{MN}(I_{NN} - A_{NN})^{-1} T_N
\tag{5.15}
$$

To define the total and first order aggregation bias, it will be helpful to write the two inverse matrices in the bracketed expression in (5.15) as power series expansions.[8] These expansions are given in (5.16) and (5.17)

$$
(I_{MM} - \hat{A}_{MM})^{-1} = (I_{MM} + \hat{A}_{MM} + \hat{A}_{MM}^2 + \ldots)
\tag{5.16}
$$

$$
(I_{NN} - A_{NN})^{-1} = (I_{NN} + A_{NN} + A_{NN}^2 + \ldots)
\tag{5.17}
$$

Next, substitute (5.16) and (5.17) into (5.15), note that $I_{MM}J_{MN} = J_{MN}I_{NN}$, and add and subtract $(A_{MM} + A_{MM}^2 + \ldots) J_{MN} T_N$. This yields

$$\hat{X}_M - X_M = \{(A_{MM} + A_{MM}^2 + \ldots)J_{MN} - J_{MN}(A_{NN} + A_{NN}^2 + \ldots)\}T_N$$
$$+ \{\hat{A}_{MM} + \hat{A}_{MM}^2 + \ldots)J_{MN} - (A_{MM} + A_{MM}^2 + \ldots)J_{MN}\}T_N$$

(5.18)

Equation (5.18) indicates that the difference between $\hat{X}_M$ and X_M depends upon two components. The first, which is $\{A_{MM} + A_{MM}^2 + \ldots)J_{MN} - J_{MN}(A_{NN} + A_{NN}^2 + \ldots)\}T_N$, may be interpreted as total aggregation bias. As should be apparent, this source of error arises because of the discrepancy between the 'true' macro coefficients and their 'true' micro counterparts. The second component, which is $\{(\hat{A}_{MM} + \hat{A}_{MM}^2 + \ldots)J_{MN} - (A_{MM} + A_{MM}^2 + \ldots)J_{MN}\}T_N$, may then be interpreted as the total estimation error. That is, due to sampling variability and to any statistical biases associated with estimating A_{MM}, the elements of $\hat{A}_{MM}$ will not, in general, be equal to their corresponding parameters.

Since it will be needed later, the concept of first order aggregation bias should also be defined before concluding this section. Essentially, this definition is necessary because equation (5.18), despite its attractive interpretation, is too complicated to be useful in the subsequent analysis. In any event, an expression for the first order aggregation bias may be obtained by neglecting all but the first order terms in $\{(A_{MM} + A_{MM}^2 + \ldots)J_{MN} - J_{MN}(A_{NN} + A_{NN}^2 + \ldots)\}T_N$. Therefore, the first order aggregation bias, denoted by P, may be defined as[9]

$$P = \{A_{MM}J_{MN} - J_{MN}A_{NN}\}T_N \tag{5.19}$$

2. THE RELATION BETWEEN FIRST ORDER AGGREGATION BIAS AND ESTIMATION TECHNIQUE

Based upon the results of the previous section, it is now possible to study the effect of different estimation techniques on the magnitude of the first order aggregation bias as defined in equation (5.19). Essentially, it will be argued that: (1) an estimator of the macro coefficients is, in part, a weighted average of underlying micro coefficients and (2) these weighted averages are different for different estimators. These facts will be used to cite the conditions for the ratio estimator of the macro coefficients to have a zero first order aggregation bias and to prove the promised theorems on eliminating first order aggregation bias under k-class estimation of A_{MM}.[10] These results will be presented in Parts B and C respectively. Before this can be done, though, a sufficient condition for the elimination of first order aggregation bias by any estimator must be given. This condition is provided in Part A.

A. A sufficient condition for zero first order aggregation bias

From equation (5.19), a sufficient condition for zero first order aggregation bias is obviously

$$A_{MM}J_{MN}T_N = J_{MN}A_{NN}T_N \tag{5.20}$$

However, an expression for (5.20) based upon the elements of these matrices is more helpful. Using the notation established in (5.7) and (5.8), this expression for the ith element on both sides of (5.20) is

$$\sum_{j=1}^{M} a_{ij} \sum_{h=S(j-1)+1}^{S(j)} \tau_h = \sum_{l=S(i-1)+1}^{S(i)} \sum_{j=1}^{M} \sum_{h=S(j-1)+1}^{S(j)} \alpha_{lh} \tau_h \tag{5.21}$$

where $i = 1, \ldots, M$ and where $S(j)$ denotes the total number of micro sectors aggregated into the first j macro sectors and where $S(0)=0$.[11] A stronger statement of the condition in (5.21), which will be useful monetarily, is

$$a_{ij}\sum_{h} \tau_h = \sum_{l}\sum_{h}\alpha_{lh}\tau_h \qquad i,j = 1, \ldots, M \tag{5.22}$$

or

$$a_{ij} = \sum_{l}\sum_{h}\alpha_{lh}\tau_h^* \qquad i,j = 1, \ldots, M \tag{5.23}$$

where $\tau_h^* = \tau_h/\sum_{h} \tau_h$. Hence, if each of the M^2 macro coefficients are equal to the particular weighted average of micro coefficients on the right-hand side of (5.23), then the first order aggregation bias will vanish.

B. The conditions for zero first order aggregation bias using the ratio estimator

Using equation (5.23), the conditions under which the ratio estimator will have zero first order aggregation bias may be investigated. In order to do so, however, the following two definitions are needed:

Definition 1: In terms of equation (5.4), the ratio estimator of the 'columns only' macro coefficients is

$$\hat{a}_{ij}(R) = \frac{\sum_r Z_{ij}^{(r)}}{\sum_r X_j^{(r)}} \tag{5.24}$$

where n_j represents the number of firms in the jth macro sector on which observations were taken.[12]

But since $Z_{ij}^{(r)}$ is just the purchases of the several goods and services produced by i for use as inputs in the several outputs produced by the rth firm in j, $\sum_r Z_{ij}^{(r)} = \sum_r \sum_l \sum_h \zeta_{lh}^{(r)}$.[13] By the same token, $\sum_r X_j^{(r)} = \sum_r \sum_h \chi_h^{(r)}$. Hence, by Definition 1,

$$\hat{a}_{ij}(R) = \frac{\sum_r \sum_l \sum_h \zeta_{lh}^{(r)}}{\sum_r \sum_h \chi_h^{(r)}} = \frac{\sum_r \sum_l \sum_h (\alpha_{lh} \chi_h^{(r)} + v_{lh}^{(r)})}{\sum_r \sum_h \chi_h^{(r)}} \tag{5.25}$$

where the extreme right-hand term of equation (5.25) is obtained from substituting equation (5.2). This prompts

Definition 2. When the macro coefficients are estimated using the ratio method, the true i,j^{th} macro coefficient may be defined as the following weighted average of underlying micro coefficients.

$$a_{ij}(R) = \frac{\sum_r \sum_l \sum_h \alpha_{lh} \chi_h^{(r)}}{\sum_r \sum_h \chi_h^{(r)}} \tag{5.26}$$

Now, the relevant condition for zero first order aggregation bias in the ratio estimator of a_{ij}, $\hat{a}_{ij}(R)$, may be set forth in Theorem 1.[14] Two interpretations of this theorem will be given in the discussion immediately following its proof.

Theorem 1. From equation (5.23), recall that if $a_{ij} = \sum_l \sum_h \alpha_{lh} \tau_h^*$ where $\tau_h^* = \tau_h / \sum_h \tau_h$, then first order aggregation bias vanishes. Further denote $\chi_h = \sum_r \chi_h^{(r)}$ and $\chi_h^* = \chi_h / \sum_h \chi_h$. Then, if for each j, $\tau_h^* = \chi_h^*$ for all h, first order aggregation bias vanishes if the ratio estimator is used to estimate the macro coefficients.

Proof: From Definition 2,

$$a_{ij}(R) = \frac{\sum_r \sum_l \sum_h \alpha_{lh} \chi_h^{(r)}}{\sum_r \sum_h \chi_h^{(r)}} \tag{5.27}$$

and from the notational conventions adopted in the theorem

$$a_{ij}(R) = \frac{\sum_l \sum_h \alpha_{lh} \chi_h}{\sum_h \chi_h^{(r)}} = \sum_l \sum_h \alpha_{lh} \chi_h^* \tag{5.28}$$

Hence, if $\chi_h^* = \tau_h^*$ for all h, then by equation (5.23)

$$a_{ij}(R) = \sum_l \sum_h \alpha_{lh} \chi_h^* = \sum_l \sum_h \alpha_{lh} \tau_h^* \tag{5.29}$$

Finally, if this condition holds for all i and j, then Theil's first order aggregation bias vanishes.

The conditions for zero first order aggregation bias utilized by equation (5.29) in the proof of Theorem 1 has at least two interpretations. First, this condition, which requires $\chi_h^* = \tau_h^*$, means that if the structure of final demands within each macro sector in the period for which the forecast is to be made is the same as the corresponding outputs included in the base period sample, then first order aggregation bias vanishes if the ratio estimator is used to estimate the macro coefficients. In other words, first order aggregation bias disappears if, for all h and j, the fraction of base period total output accounted for by micro sector h in macro sector j is equal to the forecast period fraction of final demand accounted for by micro sector h in macro sector j.[15] As a second interpretation of Theorem 1, note that $\sum_h \tau_h^* = 1$ and rewrite equation (5.29) as

$$a_{ij}(R) = a_{ij} + \sum_l \sum_h (\alpha_{lh} - a_{ij}) \tau_h^* \tag{5.30}$$

Hence, this theorem also implies that if the covariance

$$\sum_l \sum_h (\alpha_{lh} - a_{ij}) \tau_h^* = 0 \tag{5.31}$$

then first order aggregation bias vanishes under the standard ratio estimator.[16]

C. The conditions for zero first order aggregation bias using k-class estimators

In Definition 2, $a_{ij}(R)$ was specified to be a weighted average of underlying micro coefficients; a convention which is consistent with the treatment of the aggregation problem in other settings. However, it should be emphasized that these weights are peculiar to the ratio estimator. That is, if the true macro coefficients were similarly defined for another estimator, the weights attached to the micro coefficients would, in general, be different. Hence, the conditions for zero first order aggregation bias would also change.

   This idea will be explored in the remainder of this section by investigating the weights which k-class estimators assign to the underlying micro coefficients. In particular, the exposition will indicate not only that the k-class weights differ from the ratio weights, but that the k-class weights differ for all values of k. As a result of this finding, then, it will be argued that there are wide possibilities for eliminating first order aggregation bias if the appropriate member of the k-class is used to estimate the macro coefficients. Before this can be done, however, it is first necessary to review the way in which members of the k-class may be used to estimate the macro coefficients.

   In Chapter 3, it was shown that equation (5.4), which is,

$$Z_{ij}^{(r)} = a_{ij}X_{j}^{(r)} + u_{ij}^{(r)} \tag{5.4}$$

is a member of the larger system of equations in (3.16). Furthermore, it was argued that a member of the k-class may be used to estimate the a_{ij}. Specifically, this class of estimates is defined in

Definition 3. In terms of equation (3.16), k-class estimates of the macro coefficients are given by

$$\hat{a}_{ij}(k) = \frac{\sum_{r}(X_{j}^{(r)} - k\hat{w}_{j}^{(r)})\,Z_{ij}^{(r)}}{\sum_{r}(X_{j}^{(r)})^{2} - k\sum_{r}(\hat{w}_{j}^{(r)})^{2}}; k \geq 0 \tag{5.32}$$

where the $\hat{w}_{j}^{(r)}$ are the observed residuals from an ordinary least squares regression of $X_{j}^{(r)}$ on $WS_{j}^{(r)}$ and $PG_{j}^{(r)}$.

In addition, using the discussion between Definitions 1 and 2, the true macro coefficients under k-class estimation is stated in

Definition 4. When the macro coefficients are estimated by a member of the k-class, the true i,j^{th} macro coefficient is given by the following weighted average of underlying micro coefficients

$$a_{ij}(k) = \frac{\sum_r (X_j^{(r)} - k\hat{w}_j^{(r)}) \sum_l \sum_h \alpha_{lh} X_h^{(r)}}{\sum_r (X_j^{(r)})^2 - k \sum_r (\hat{w}_j^{(r)})^2} \tag{5.33}$$

Based upon these two definitions, a set of sufficient conditions for eliminating first order aggregation bias using k-class estimators for the macro coefficients may be stated. These conditions, which are analogous to those contained in Theorem 1, are given Theorem 2. An interpretation of this theorem will be presented immediately following its proof.

Theorem 2. Let a_{ij} be given by equation (5.23) and let $\hat{\gamma}_h(k)$ be a k-class estimate of γ_h; the slope coefficient from an auxiliary regression of $\chi_h^{(r)}$ on $X_j^{(r)}$. Then, if for each i and j, $\sum \sum (\alpha_{lh} - a_{ij}) \gamma_h(k) = 0$ for some $k \geq 0$, first order aggregation bias vanishes if that member of the k-class is used to estimate the macro coefficients.

Proof: From Definition 4

$$a_{ij}(k) = \frac{\sum_r (X_j^{(r)} - k\hat{w}_j^{(r)}) \sum_l \sum_h \alpha_{lh} X_h^{(r)}}{\sum_r (X_j^{(r)})^2 - k \sum_r (\hat{w}_j^{(r)})^2} \tag{5.34}$$

Upon rearranging terms, (5.34) becomes

$$= \sum_l \sum_h \alpha_{lh} \left[\frac{\sum_r (X_j^{(r)} - k\hat{w}_j^{(r)}) \chi_h^{(r)}}{\sum_r (X_j^{(r)})^2 - k \sum_r (\hat{w}_j^{(r)})^2} \right] \tag{5.35}$$

Now, the term in brackets should be recognized as a k-class estimate of the auxiliary regression coefficient γ_h. Hence, since it can be easily verified that $\sum_h \hat{\gamma}_h(k) = 1$,

$$a_{ij}(k) = \sum_l \sum_h \alpha_{lh} \hat{\gamma}_h(k) = a_{ij} + \sum_l \sum_h (\alpha_{lh} - a_{ij}) \hat{\gamma}_h(k) \tag{5.36}$$

Therefore, if for each i and j the covariance between $(\alpha_{lh} - a_{ij})$ and $\hat{\gamma}_h(k)$ is equal to zero for all l, first order aggregation bias disappears if the appropriate member of the k-class is used to estimate the macro coefficients.

Admittedly, it is difficult to attach an intuitive explanation for the condition

$$\sum_l \sum_h (\alpha_{lh} - a_{ij})\hat{\gamma}_h(k) = 0 \tag{5.37}$$

which was necessary to prove Theorem 2. However, a special case of this theorem is somewhat easier to interpret. That is, suppose that the multiple correlation between $X_j^{(r)}$ and the variables $WS_j^{(r)}$ and $PG_j^{(r)}$ is close to unity.[17] Then, by Definition 4, the $\hat{w}_j^{(r)}$, which are the observed residuals from an ordinary least squares regression of $X_j^{(r)}$ on $WS_j^{(r)}$ and $PG_j^{(r)}$, will be nearly zero. Under this circumstance, $\hat{\gamma}_h(k)$ may be approximated by

$$\hat{\gamma}_h(k) \approx \frac{\sum_r X_j^{(r)} X_h^{(r)}}{\sum_r (X_j^{(r)})^2} \tag{5.38}$$

Finally, substituting the approximation in (5.38) into (5.36) produces

$$a_{ij}(k) = a_{ij} + \sum_l \sum_h (\alpha_{lh} - a_{ij}) \frac{\sum_r X_j^{(r)} X_h^{(r)}}{\sum_r (X_j^{(r)})^2} \tag{5.39}$$

or

$$a_{ij}(k) = a_{ij} + \frac{\sum_r X_j^{(r)}}{\sum_r (X_j^{(r)})^2} \sum_l \sum_h (\alpha_{lh} - a_{ij}) X_h^{(r)} \tag{5.40}$$

Therefore, if the covariance between $(\alpha_{lh} - a_{ij})$ and $X_h^{(r)}$ is equal to zero for all l and r, then

$$\frac{\sum_r X_j^{(r)}}{\sum_r (X_j^{(r)})^2} \sum_l \sum_h (\alpha_{lh} - a_{ij}) X_h^{(r)} = 0 \tag{5.41}$$

and first order aggregation bias vanishes in this special case of Theorem 2. It should be apparent, upon inspecting equation (5.41), that this result holds regardless of which member of the k-class was used to estimate the macro coefficients.

Theorem 2, though, is deficient in at least one respect. That is, it gives the conditions for zero first order aggregation bias in terms of a set of regression coefficients; the $\hat{\gamma}_h(k)$. However, since k-class estimators are defined only for $k \geq 0$, the following theorem is needed to define the conditions under which a suitable k may be selected and to show how this value may be found.

Theorem 3. If (1) $\sum_l \sum_h (\alpha_{lh} - a_{ij}) \sum_r X_j^{(r)} X_h^{(r)} \geq 0$

and $\sum_l \sum_h (\alpha_{lh} - a_{ij}) \sum_r \hat{w}_j^{(r)} X_h^{(r)} > 0$

or (2) $\sum_l \sum_h (\alpha_{lh} - a_{ij}) \sum_r X_j^{(r)} X_h^{(r)} \leq 0$

and $\sum_l \sum_h (\alpha_{lh} - a_{ij}) \sum_r \hat{w}_j^{(r)} X_h^{(r)} < 0$ then there exists a member of
the k-class which will eliminate the first order aggregation bias on the i, j^{th} macro coefficient provided that this choice of k does not make

$$\sum_r (X_j^{(r)})^2 - k\sum_r (w_j^{(r)})^2 = 0.$$

Furthermore, if it exists, this member may be found from the formula

$$k = \left[\frac{\sum_l \sum_h (\alpha_{lh} - a_{ij}) \sum_r X_j^{(r)} X_h^{(r)}}{\sum_l \sum_h (\alpha_{lh} - a_{ij}) \sum_r \hat{w}_j^{(r)} X_h^{(r)}} \right]$$

Proof. For zero first order aggregation bias, Theorem 2 requires that

$$\sum_l \sum_h (\alpha_{lh} - a_{ij}) \left[\frac{\sum_r (X_j^{(r)} - k\hat{w}_j^{(r)}) X_h^{(r)}}{\sum_r (X_j^{(r)})^2 - k\sum_r (\hat{w}_j^{(r)})^2} \right] = 0 \qquad (5.42)$$

But since $\sum_r (X_j^{(r)})^2 - k\sum_r (\hat{w}_j^{(r)})^2 \neq 0$, then this is equivalent to

$$\sum_l \sum_h (\alpha_{lh} - a_{ij}) \sum_r (X_j^{(r)} - k\hat{w}_j^{(r)}) X_h^{(r)} = 0 \qquad (5.43)$$

or

$$k = \frac{\sum_l \sum_h (\alpha_{lh} - a_{ij}) \sum_r X_j^{(r)} X_h^{(r)}}{\sum_l \sum_h (\alpha_{lh} - a_{ij}) \sum_r \hat{w}_j^{(r)} X_h^{(r)}} \qquad (5.44)$$

Therefore, if this ratio of covariances is non-negative, then a member of the k-class exists for which the estimate of the i, j^{th} macro coefficient will have zero first order aggregation bias. In addition, if it exists, this member may be found from equation (5.44).

Three interesting corollaries follow from Theorem 3 which are obvious and may be stated without proof.

Corollary 1. Given the conditions of Theorem 3, if

$$\sum_l \sum_h (\alpha_{lh} - a_{ij}) \sum X_j^{(r)} X_h^{(r)} = 0,$$

then ordinary least squares is the member of the k-class which eliminates first order aggregation bias in the estimate of the i, j^{th} macro coefficient. It should be noted, however, that if ordinary least squares is used to estimate the macro coefficients, the resulting estimates will be biased and inconsistent in the usual statistical sense.

Corollary 2. Given the conditions of Theorem 3, if

$$\sum_l \sum_h (\alpha_{lh} - a_{ij}) \sum X_j^{(r)} X_h^{(r)} = \sum_l \sum_h (\alpha_{lh} - a_{ij}) \sum \hat{w}_j^{(r)} X_h^{(r)}$$

then two-stage least squares is the member of the k-class which eliminates first order aggregation bias in the estimate of the i, j^{th} macro coefficient.

Finally, Mariano and Sawa have shown that k-class estimators possess moments of order greater than or equal to unity if and only if $0 \le k \le 1$.[18] This prompts the self-evident

Corollary 3. Given the conditions in Theorem 3, if

$$\left| \sum_l \sum_h (\alpha_{lh} - a_{ij}) \sum X_j^{(r)} X_h^{(r)} \right| \le \left| \sum_l \sum_h (\alpha_{lh} - a_{ij}) \sum_r \hat{w}_j^{(r)} X_h^{(r)} \right|$$

then the member of the k-class which eliminates first order aggregation bias in the i, j^{th} macro coefficient possesses moments of order greater than or equal to unity.

This chapter has shown that the possibilities for eliminating first order aggregation bias from estimates of the macro coefficients are much wider than is generally realized. That is, if a member of the k-class which satisfies the conditions presented in Theorem 2 is used, then this source of error can be made to disappear. However, equation (5.19) demonstrated that aggregation bias is not the only source of error in an input-output forecast. Estimation error will also be present. Furthermore, this second source of error is also influenced by the choice of an estimator for the macro coefficients. For example, as has been well-established, the mean square error associated with ordinary least squares estimates of parameters in a simultaneous equations system exceeds its counterpart for two-stage least squares. As a result, eliminating first order aggregation bias may be possible only if an analyst is willing to accept an increased level of estimation error.

NOTES

1. For example, see Kenjiro Ara, 'The Aggregation Problem in Input-Output Analysis,' *Econometrica*, XXVII, April, 1959; Michio Hatanaka, 'A Note on Consolidation Within a Leontief System,' *Econometrica*, XX, April, 1952; Yoshinori Morimoto, 'On Aggregation Problems in Input-Output Analysis,' *Review of Economic Studies*, XXXVII (1), January, 1970; and Henri Theil, 'Linear Aggregation in Input-Output Analysis,' *Econometrica*, XXV, January, 1957. For a more complete listing of the better known works in this area, consult the bibliography.
2. Theil, 'Linear Aggregation.' It might be noted that elimination of first order aggregation bias does not constitute elimination of total aggregation bias. The distinction between these two concepts will be made explicit shortly.
3. Theil, 'Linear Aggregation' and Morimoto, 'On Aggregation Problems.'
4. Recall that a more complete discussion of random disturbances in input-output relations are given in Chapters 2 and 3.
5. Note that equation (5.2) contains no statement about which technique ought to be used to estimate the α_{lh}. As was mentioned, in the introduction, both the ratio and the k-class techniques will be considered, but this will be done at a later point in the chapter. In addition, equation (5.2) will produce 'columns only' estimates of the α_{lh}. The aggregation bias arising from 'rows only' estimates are ignored in this chapter.
6. In the analysis to follow, the subscript refers to the order of the vector or matrix in question. For example, in equation (5.5), X_N is $Nx1$ and A_{NN} is NxN.
7. The discussion in the remainder of this section closely follows Theil, 'Linear Aggregation,' p. 114. It should be noted that Theil's focus was exclusively upon deriving an expression for aggregation bias.
8. Fredrick Waugh, 'Inversion of the Leontief Matrix by a Power Series,' *Econometrica*, XVIII, April, 1950.
9. This definition of first order aggregation bias was first given in Theil, 'Linear Aggregation,' p. 117.
10. It should be recalled that the ratio estimator for the macro coefficients was discussed in Section 2 of Chapter 3.
11. To economize on notation, in the remainder of this chapter denote

$$\sum_{l=S(i-1)+1}^{S(i)} = \sum_l,$$

$$\text{and} \sum_{h=S(j-1)+1}^{S(j)} = \sum_h.$$

In addition,

$$\sum_{r=1}^{n_j}$$

where n_j is the sample size in sector j, is simplified as $\sum_r$.

12. No distinction is made as to the micro sectors from which these firms are drawn.
13. Henceforth, it is assumed that once the micro sectors have been aggregated into macro sectors, the firms in question are appropriately renumbered. This implies that variables such as ζ_{lh} may be summed over r.
14. For a closely related theorem, Yoshinori Morimoto, 'On Aggregation Problems,' p. 121.
15. *Ibid.*
16. Actually, the condition for eliminating first order aggregation bias in the ratio estimator as given in equation (5.31) was stated and proved as a theorem by Theil, 'Linear Aggregation.'
17. Recall that in Chapter 3, $WS_j^{(r)}$ and $PG_j^{(r)}$ denoted, respectively, wages and salaries and payments to government. Since both variables are exogenous variables in (3.16), they are used in the auxiliary regression just described.
18. Roberto S. Mariano and Takamitsu Sawa, 'The Exact Finite Sample Distribution of the Limited Information Maximum Likelihood Estimator in the Case of Two Endogenous Variables,' *Journal of the American Statistical Association*, LXVII, March, 1972, p. 161–62.

6. A postscript

As was indicated in Chapter 1, this monograph had two principle objectives. The first, and most important, of these was to develop a method for determining the 'goodness of fit' between an input-output model and data from the real world. To accomplish this goal, it was demonstrated in Chapter 3 that two-stage least squares may be used to estimate the technical coefficients. Specifically, if this technique is employed, consistent estimates of these parameters and asymptotic standard errors for these estimates may be obtained. In addition, Chapter 3 provided an illustration of this estimation technique using cross-sectional data from twenty-nine sectors of the West Virginia economy. Although they are based solely upon 'columns only' information, these results at least cast some doubt upon the effectiveness of the input-output approach. That is, once the data were adjusted for heteroskedasticity, only about 36% of the coefficient estimates could pass a 5% significance test.

The second objective, then, was to suggest three further uses of the two-stage least squares estimation technique in an input-output context. First, as an improvement over current methods for reconciling 'rows only' and 'columns only' estimates for the technical coefficients, the following two-step procedure was recommended in Section 1 of Chapter 4: (1) Use two-stage least squares to calculate estimates for both types of technical coefficients and (2) apply the standard theorems on linear combinations of random variable in order to produce the minimum variance combined estimator. Second, in Section 2 of Chapter 4, a more systematic method for selecting sample sizes in future input-output studies was presented. Since this method is also based upon the minimum variance principle, it closely resembles its counterpart in the literature on stratified sampling. Finally, the problem of aggregation bias in input-output models was studied in Chapter 5. This chapter demonstrated that: (1) the size of the aggregation bias is directly related to the econometric technique used to estimate the technical coefficients and, as a consequence, (2) if the appropriate estimator is used, a large part of this source of error may vanish.

The above results, however, were not obtained without cost. To calculate standard errors for the estimated technical coefficients, it was necessary to assume that all firms in each sector have identical Leontief type production functions. Admittedly, this assumption is restrictive. Furthermore, it will be violated in many practical situations as most input-output sectors are composed of firms producing a wide range of products. However, the reader should keep in mind that this assumption makes it possible to obtain valuable information which can be used to improve the quality of survey based input-output studies.

Hopefully, other researchers will choose to pursue this line of investigation as there is a great deal which remains to be done. For example, now that econometric methods for estimating the technical coefficients have been established, more complete tests of input-output models might be performed. As an illustration of how this could be done, consider the following simulation experiment. First, take an existing survey based input-output model, express it in matrix form as

$$X(t) = AX(t) + Y(t) \tag{6.1}$$

and re-estimate the technical coefficients by two-stage least squares. Second, specify a final demand vector for some future year (say, $t + s$). Third, 'shock' the A matrix by adding a matrix of random elements. By the asymptotic properties of A, the i, j^{th} random element might reasonably be assumed to be normally distributed with zero mean and variance $\sigma_{\hat{a}_{ij}}$. Fourth, after adding the matrix of disturbances to A, put the system shown in (6.1) into reduced form and derive the resulting estimates of $X(t + s)$. Fifth, repeat steps three and four as often as desired in order to calculate the moments of the empirical sampling distribution for $X(t + s)$.

This possibility for an empirical studies is meant only to be illustrative. In addition, such a study will certainly raise further questions about the effectiveness of input-output models in representing economic systems. But until an investigation of this type is carried out, many of the issues raised in this monograph will be left unresolved. In particular, since large amounts of money are currently spent to implement input-output models, some answers, even though they may only be tentative, are in order.

Bibliography

Adams, A. A., and I. G. Stewart, 'Input-Output Analysis: An Application,' *The Economic Journal*, LXVI, No. 263, September, 1956, p. 442–454.

Ara, Kenjiro, 'The Aggregation Problem in Input-Output Analysis,' *Econometrica*, XXVII, No. 2, April, 1959, p. 257–62.

Arrow, Kenneth J., and Marvin Hoffenberg, *A Time Series Analysis of Interindustry Demands*, Amsterdam, North-Holland, 1959.

Arrow, Kenneth J., 'Alternative Proof of the Substitution Theorem for Leontief Models in the General Case,' *Activity Analysis of Production and Allocation*, ed. Tjalling C. Koopmans, New York, John Wiley and Sons, 1951.

Babbar, M. M., 'Distribution of Solution of a Set of Linear Equations (with an Application to Linear Programming),' *Journal of the American Statistical Association*, L, No. 271, September, 1955, p. 854–69.

Bacharach, Michael, *Biproportional Matrices and Input-Output Change*, Cambridge, Cambridge University Press, 1970.

Bailey, William R., 'A Note on the 1947 Input-Output Study,' *Review of Economics and Statistics*, L, No. 1, February, 1968, p. 138–140.

Balderson, Judith, 'Models of General Equilibrium,' *Economic Activity Analysis*, ed. Oskar Morgenstern, New York, John Wiley and Sons, 1954.

Barnett, Harold J., 'Specific Industry Output Projections,' *Long Range Economic Projection: Studies in Income and Wealth*, ed. National Bureau of Economic Research, Princeton, Princeton University Press, 1954.

Beyers, William B., 'On the Stability of Regional Interindustry Models: The Washington Data for 1963 and 1967,' *Journal of Regional Science*, XII, No. 3, December, 1972, p. 363–374.

Billings, R. Bruce, 'Regional Defense Impact–A Case Study Comparison of Measurement Techniques,' *Journal of Regional Science*, X, No. 2, August, 1970, p. 199–216.

Bose, Sanjit, 'A New Proof of the Non-Substitution Theorem,' *International Economic Review*, XIII, No. 1, February, 1972, p. 182–186.

Bourque, Phillip J., *et al.*, *The Washington Economy: An Input-Output Study*, Seattle, Washington, University of Washington, 1967.

Bradley, Iver E., and James P. Gander, 'Input-Output Multipliers: Some Theoretical Comments,' *Journal of Regional Science*, IX, No. 2, August, 1969, p. 309–317.

Bradwell, David; Leonard Kunin, and Everard Lofting, 'An Interindustry Analysis of the San Francisco Bay Region with Emphasis on Environmental Impact,' *American Statistical Association, Proceedings*, 1971, p. 90–98.

Briggs, F. E. A., 'On Problems of Estimation in Leontief Models,' *Econometrica*, XXV, No. 2, July, 1957, p. 444–55.

Cameron, Burgess, 'The Production Function in Leontief Models,' *The Review of Economic Studies*, XX (1), No. 51, 1952–1953, p. 62–69.

Carter, Ann P., *Structural Change in the American Economy*, Cambridge, Mass., Harvard University Press, 1970.

Chenery, Hollis B. and Tsunehiko Watanabe, 'International Comparisons of the Structure of Production,' *Econometrica*, XXVI, No. 4, October, 1958, p. 487–521.

Chenery, Hollis, B. and Paul G. Clark, *Interindustry Economics*, New York, John Wiley and Sons, 1959.

Christ, Carl F., 'A Review of Input-Output Analysis,' *Input-Output Analysis: An Appraisal*, ed. National Bureau of Economic Research. Princeton University Press, 1957.
Czamanski, Stanislaw and Emil E. Malizia, 'Applicability and Limitations in the Use of National Input-Output Tables for Regional Studies,' *The Regional Science Association Papers*, XXIII, 1969, p. 65–78.

Department of Applied Economics, University of Cambridge, "A Computable Model of Economic Growth,' *A Programme for Growth*, ed. Richard Stone, London, Chapman-Hall, 1962.
Department of Applied Economics, University of Cambridge, 'Input-Output Relationships, 1954–1966,' *A Programme for Growth*, ed. Richard Stone, London, Chapman and Hall, 1963.
Dhrymes, Phoebus, J., *Econometrics: Statistical Foundations and Applications*, New York, Harper and Row, 1970.
Dorfman, Robert, Paul A. Samuelson, and Robert M. Solow, *Linear Programming and Economic Analysis*, New York, McGraw-Hill, 1958.

Eckstein, Otto, 'The Input-Output System–Its Nature and Use,' *Economic Activity Analysis*, ed. Oskar Morgenstern, New York, John Wiley and Sons, 1954.
Emerson, Jarvin, 'An Interindustry Comparison of Regional and National Economic Structure,' *The Regional Science Association Papers*, XXVI, 1972, p. 164–177.

Fei, John Ching-Han, 'A Fundamental Theorem for the Aggregation Problem of Input-Output Analysis,' *Econometrica*, XXIV, No. 4, October, 1956, p. 400–12.
Fisher, Franklin M., *The Identification Problem in Econometrics*, New York, McGraw-Hill, 1966.
Fisher, Walter D., 'Criteria for Aggregation in Input-Output Analysis,' *Review of Economics and Statistics*, XL, No. 3, August, 1958, p. 250–260.
Forssell, Osmo, 'Explaining Changes in Input-Output Coefficients for Finland,' *Input-Output Techniques*, ed. A. P. Carter and A. Brody, Amsterdam, North-Holland, 1972.

Glazer, Ezra, 'Interindustry Economics Research,' *The American Statistician*, V, No. 2, April–May, 1951, p. 9–11.
Green, R. Jeffery, 'Alternative Significance Tests for TSLS Estimated Parameters: Some Monte Carlo Evidence,' *Metroeconomica*, XXV, No. 2, May–August, 1973, p. 183–93.
Goldfeld, Steven M. and Quandt, Richard E., 'Some Tests for Homoskedasticity,' *Journal of the American Statistical Association*, LX, No. 310, September, 1965, p. 539–47.
Gordon, S. L., and I. R. Edwards, 'The Application of Input-Output Methods to Regional Forecasting: The British Experience,' *Regional Forecasting*, ed. Michael Chisholm, Allan E. Frey and Peter Haggett, London, Butterworths, 1970.

Hansen, Morris H., William N. Hurwitz, and William G. Madow, *Sample Survey Methods and Theory*, Vol. I, New York, John Wiley and Sons, 1953.
Hansen, W. Lee, and Charles M. Tiebout, 'An Intersectoral Flows Analysis of the California Economy,' *Review of Economics and Statistics*, XLV, No. 4, November, 1963, p. 409–418.
Hatanaka, Michio, 'A Note on Consolidation Within a Leontief System,' *Econometrica*, XX, No. 2, April, 1952, p. 301–303.
Hirsch, Werner Z., *Urban Economic Analysis*, New York, McGraw-Hill, 1973.
Hirsch, Werner Z., 'Interindustry Relations of a Metropolitan Area,' *Review of Economics and Statistics*, XLI, No. 4, November, 1959, p. 360–369.
Hochwald, Werner; Herbert E. Striner, and Sidney Sonenblum, *Local Impact of Foreign Trade*, Washington, D.C., National Planning Association, 1960.
Hurwicz, Leonid, 'Input-Output Analysis and Economic Structure: A Review Article,' *American Economic Review*, XLV, No. 4, September, 1955, p. 626–636.

Isard, Walter and Thomas Langford, *Regional Input-Output Study: Recollections, Reflections and Diverse Notes on the Philadelphia Experience*, Cambridge, Mass., MIT Press, 1971.

Johnston, J., *Econometric Methods*, Second revised edition, New York, McGraw-Hill, 1972.

Karaska, Gerald, J., 'Variation of Input-Output Coefficients for Different Levels of Aggregation,' *Journal of Regional Science*, VIII, No. 2, Winter, 1968, p. 215–227.

Klein, Lawrence R., *A Textbook of Econometrics*, Evanston, Illinois, Row, Peterson and Co., 1953.

Klein, Lawrence, *A Textbook of Econometrics*, Second edition revised, Englewood Cliffs, New Jersey, Prentice-Hall, 1974.

Koopmans, Tjalling C., 'Alternative Proof of the Substitution Theorem for Leontief Models in the Case of Three Industries,' *Activity Analysis of Production and Allocation*, ed. Tjalling C. Koopmans, New York, John Wiley and Sons, 1951.

Koopmans, Tjalling C., *Three Essays on the State of Economic Science*, McGraw-Hill, New York, 1957.

Kossov, V., 'The Theory of Aggregation in Input-Output Models,' *Contributions to Input-Output Analysis*, ed. A. P. Carter and A. Brody, Amsterdam, North-Holland, 1970.

Lee, Tong Hun; R. John Moore, and David P. Lewis, *A Report on the Tennessee Interindustry Study*, Knoxville, Tenn., University of Tennessee Press, 1967.

Leontief, Wassily, 'Recent Developments in the Study of Interindustrial Relationships,' *American Economic Review*, XXXIX, No. 3, May, 1949, p. 211–225.

Leontief, Wassily W., *The Structure of the American Economy: 1919–1935*, New York, Oxford University Press, 1951.

Leontief, Wassily, 'Some Basic Problems of Empirical Input-Output Analysis,' *Input-Output Analysis: An Appraisal*, ed. National Bureau of Economic Research, Princeton, Princeton University Press, 1955.

Leontief, Wassily; Alice Morgan; Karne Polenske; David Simpson; and Edward Tower, 'The Economic Impact-Industrial and Regional- of an Arms Cut,' *Review of Economics and Statistics*, XLVII, No. 3, August, 1965, p. 217–241.

Leontief, Wassily, 'Environmental Repercussions and Economic Growth,' *Review of Economics and Statistics*, LII, No. 3, August, 1970, p. 262–271.

Long, Neal B., Jr., 'An Input-Output Comparison of the Economic Structure of the US and the USSR,' *Review of Economics and Statistics*, LII, No. 4, November, 1970, p. 434–441.

Long, Wesley H., 'An Examination of Linear Homogeneity of Trade and Production Functions in County Leontief Matrices,' *Journal of Regional Science*, IX, No. 1, April, 1969, p. 47–69.

McGilvray, James and David Simpson, 'Some Tests of Stability in Interindustry Coefficients,' *Econometrica*, XXXVII, No. 2, April, 1969, p. 204–221.

McManus, M., 'General Consistent Aggregation in Leontief Models,' *Yorkshire Bulletin of Economic and Social Research*, VIII, No. 1, June, 1956, p. 28–48.

Malinvaud, Edmond, 'Aggregation Problems in Input-Output Models,' *The Structural Interdependence of the Economy*, ed. Tibor Barna, New York, John Wiley and Sons, 1955.

Mariano, Roberto S. and Takamitsu Sawa, 'The Exact Finite Sample Distribution of the Limited Information Maximum Likelihood Estimator in the Case of Two Endogenous Variables,' *Journal of the American Statistical Association*, LXVII, No. 337, March, 1972, p. 159–63.

Matuszewski, T. I., P. R. Pitts, and John A. Sawyer, 'Linear Programming Estimates of Changes in Input Coefficients,' *Canadian Journal of Economics and Political Science*, XXX, No. 2, May, 1964, p. 203–210.

Middlehoek, A. J., 'Tests of the Marginal Stability of Input-Output Coefficients,' *Applications of Input-Output Analysis*, ed. A. P. Carter and A. Brody, Amsterdam, North-Holland, 1970.

Miernyk, William H., *The Elements of Input-Output Analysis*, New York, Random House, 1965.

Miernyk, William H., 'Sampling Techniques in Making Regional Industry Forecasts,' *Applications of Input-Output Analysis*, ed. by A. P. Carter and A. Brody, Amsterdam, North-Holland, 1970.

Miernyk, William H., *et. al.*, *Simulating Regional Economic Development*, Lexington, Mass., D.C. Heath, 1970.

Morimoto, Yoshinori, 'On Aggregation Problems in Input-Output Analysis,' *Review of Economic Studies*, XXXVII (1), No. 109, January, 1970, p. 119–26.

Morimoto, Yoshinori, 'A Note on Weighted Aggregation in Input-Output Analysis,' *International Economic Review*, XII, No. 1, February, 1971, p. 138–143.

Moses, Leon, 'The Stability of Interregional Trading Patterns in Input-Output Analysis,' *American Economic Review*, XLV, No. 5, December, 1955, p. 803–832.

Neudecker, H., 'Aggregation in Input-Output Analysis: An Extension of Fisher's Method,' *Econometrica*, XXXVIII, No. 6, November, 1970, p. 921–26.

Ozaki, Iwao, 'Economies of Scale and Input-Output Coefficients,' *Applications of Input-Output Analysis*, ed. A. P. Carter and A. Brody, Amsterdam, North-Holland, 1970.

Peterson, Richard S. and Charles M. Tiebout, 'Measuring the Impact of Regional Defense-Space Expenditures,' *Review of Economics and Statistics*, XLVI, No. 4, November, 1964, p. 421–428.

Quandt, Richard E., 'Probabilistic Errors in the Leontief System,' *Naval Research Logistics Quarterly*, V, No. 2, July, 1958, p. 155–170.

Quandt, Richard E., 'On the Solution of Probabilistic Leontief Systems,' *Naval Research Logistics Quarterly*, VI, No. 4, December, 1959, p. 295–305.

Rasmussen, P. N., *Studies in Inter-sectoral Relations*, Amsterdam, North-Holland, 1956.

Rey, Guido and C. B. Tilanus, 'Input-Output Forecasts for the Netherlands, 1949–58,' *Econometrica*, XXXI, No. 3, July, 1963, p. 454–63.

Riefler, Roger and Charles M. Tiebout, 'Interregional Input-Output: An Empirical California-Washington Model, *Journal of Regional Science*, X, No. 2, August, 1970, p. 135–52.

Richardson, Harry, *Input-Output and Regional Economics*, New York, John Wiley and Sons, 1972.

Samuelson, Paul A., 'Abstract of a Theorem Concerning Substitution in Open Leontief Systems,' *Activity Analysis of Production and Allocation*, ed. Tjalling C. Koopmans, New York, John Wiley and Sons, 1951.

Santhanam, K. V. and R. H. Patil, 'A Study of the Production Structure of the Indian Economy: An International Comparison,' *Econometrica*, XV, No. 1, January, 1972, p. 159–176.

Schaffer, William A., and Kong Chu, 'Nonsurvey Techniques for Constructing Regional Interindustry Models,' *The Regional Science Association Papers*, XXIII, 1969, p. 83–101.

Sevaldson, Per, 'Changes in Input-Output Coefficients,' *Structural Interdependence and Economic Development*, ed. Tibor Barna, New York, St. Martin's Press, 1963.

Sevaldson, Per, 'The Stability of Input-Output Coefficients,' *Applications of Input-Output Analysis*, ed. A. P. Carter and A. Brody, Amsterdam, North-Holland, 1970.

Solow, Robert, 'On the Structure of Linear Models,' *Econometrica*, XX, No. 1, January, 1952, p. 29–46.

Stone, Richard, 'Consistent Projections in Multi-Sector Models,' *Activity Analysis in the Theory of Growth and Planning*. ed. by E. Malinvaud and M. O. L. Bacharach, New York, St. Martin's Press, 1967.

Theil, Henri, 'Linear Aggregation in Input-Output Analysis,' *Econometrica*, XXV, No. 1, January, 1957, p. 111–122.

Theil, Henri, 'The Aggregation Implications of Identifiable Structural Macro-relations,' *Econometrica*, XXVII, No. 1, January, 1959, p. 14–29.

Tiebout, Charles M., 'Regional and Interregional Input-Output Models: An Appraisal,' *Southern Economic Journal*, XXIV, No. 2, October, 1957, p. 140–147.

Tiebout, Charles M., 'An Empirical Regional Input-Output Projection Model: The State of Washington 1980,' *Review of Economics and Statistics*, LI, No. 3, August, 1969, p. 334–340.

Tilanus, C. B. and Guido Rey, 'Input-Output Volume and Value Predictions for the Netherlands, 1948–1958,' *International Economic Review*, V, No. 1, January, 1964, p. 34–45.

Tilanus, C. B., and H. Theil, 'The Information Approach to the Evaluation of Input-Output Forecasts,' *Econometrica*, XXXII, No. 4, October, 1965, p. 847–862.

Tilanus, C. B., and R. Harkema, 'Input-Output Predictions of Primary Demand, The Netherlands, 1948–1958,' *Review of Economics and Statistics*, XLVIII, No. 1, February, 1966, p. 94–97.

Tilanus, C. B., *Input-Output Experiments: The Netherlands, 1948–1961*, Rotterdam, Rotterdam University Press, 1966.

Tilanus, C. B., 'Marginal Versus Average Input Coefficients in Input-Output Forecasting,' *Quarterly Journal of Economics*, LXXXI, No. 1, February, 1967, p. 140–145.

Tomlin, Paul H., 'An Error Model for Projected Gross Outputs Using an Input-Output Model', Bureau of Census Research, Memorandum No. 212, 1973.

Tomlin, Paul H.,' Input-Output Error Analysis – Present Status,' Bureau of Census Research, Memorandum No. 317, 1973.

Walderhaug, Albert J., 'State Input-Output Tables Derived from National Data,' *American Statistical Association, Proceedings*, 1971, p. 77–89.

Waugh, Fredrick V., 'Inversion of the Leontief Matrix by a Power Series,' *Econometrica*, XVIII, No. 2, April, 1950, p. 142–54.

Studies in applied regional science

Vol. 1
On the use of input-output models for regional planning
W. A. Schaffer

This volume is devoted to the use of input-output techniques in regional planning. The study provides a clear
introduction to the essential ideas of input-output analysis.
Particular emphasis is placed on the intricate problems of
data collection at a regional level.
Attention is focused on the applicability of input-output
analysis in the field of regional planning. Alternative
methods such as shift-and-share techniques are discussed.
For means of clear illustration an extensive regional study
of the Georgia economy has been capably employed.

ISBN 90 207 0626 8

Vol. 2
Forecasting transportation impacts upon land use
P. F. Wendt (Ed.)

This reader concentrates on transportation problems in
urban areas. After a survey of model techniques for
analyzing transportation and land use problems, several
new methods in the field of transportation and land-use
planning (including Delphi-methods and interaction
models) are developed. In the study particular attention
is paid to forecasting techniques for regional-urban developments. The book is exemplified by an extensive set of
applied methods in transportation land-use planning for
the Georgia region.

ISBN 90 207 0627 6

Martinus Nijhoff Social Sciences Division, Leiden 1976

Vol. 3
Estimation of stochastic input-output models
S. D. Gerking

The primary objective of this monograph is to develop a method for measuring the uncertainty in estimates of the technical coefficients in an input-output model. Specifically, it is demonstrated that if two-stage least squares is used to estimate these parameters, then uncertainty may be judged according to the magnitude of the standard errors of these estimates.

This study also describes three further applications of the two-stage least squares estimation technique in an input-output context. The techniques and applications are illustrated using cross-sectional input-output data from West Virginia.

ISBN 90 207 0628 4